GET AHEAD
and
STAY AHEAD

GET AHEAD
and
STAY AHEAD

Use the Secrets of Your Own Brain to
Unleash Your Success at Work

NORA SIMPSON

TRUE DIRECTIONS
AN AFFILIATE OF TARCHER BOOKS

iUniverse®

GET AHEAD AND STAY AHEAD
USE THE SECRETS OF YOUR OWN BRAIN TO UNLEASH YOUR SUCCESS AT WORK

iUniverse books may be ordered through booksellers or by contacting:

iUniverse
1663 Liberty Drive
Bloomington, IN 47403
www.iuniverse.com
1-800-Authors (1-800-288-4677)

ISBN: 978-1-4917-6230-1 (sc)
ISBN: 978-1-4917-6229-5 (hc)
ISBN: 978-1-4917-6228-8 (e)

Library of Congress Control Number: 2015903395

Print information available on the last page.

iUniverse rev. date: 8/5/2015

Acknowledgments

There are many, many people who made this book possible. Just a few of them include Julia Miller, John Martin-Alexander, Jacob Waldman, Aaron Mandelbaum, Tim Gannon, my beloved Michael Brus, and my dear, wonderful Dad (Joel Simpson).

There are even more people who made the events of this book possible.

My parents gave me love, life, passion and curiosity through the hardest and the easiest of times. Mom, Dad, Marc, your courage, your humor and your unfailing commitments to self-discovery and growth have shaped my deepest self in the best ways. I am eternally grateful to you—Alice Weiss, Joel Simpson (again), and Marc Weiss—for our past, our present and our future. I love you all so much.

My sister has brought delight, joy, and affection into my life since the very first day that she was born. Molly Simpson, as long as you walk the earth, I know I will never be alone. I love and treasure you so much.

There is a special class of dear friends who have traveled the road of creativity and exploration with me, who move and enlighten me in countless ways. I am honored and delighted to know and love Leon Bynum, Damian Norfleet, Jonathan Vatner, Jamie Lawrence, Eric Mangold, Donald Wall, Marilyn Kane, Joscelyne Wilmouth, and again my beloved Michael Brus.

And then there are the amazing people—teachers, mentors, guides, friends, clients, bosses, co-workers—who've known me through the ups and downs, who've hired me, fired me, and inspired me. These folks have shared their wisdom, their strength, their problems, their fears, their hearts. They've helped me learn and grow in countless ways. My journey would not have been possible without Lynn Felsen, Sharon Siodmak, Robert Friedland, Steve Niss, Lou Sumin, Rona Davis,

Laura Sweeney, Elise Flakoll, Craig Shepard, Barry Keating, Mary Lee Amendolia, Kate Comerford, Elizabeth Waterman, June Deuell, Rick Fierstein, Kara Buller, Beth Suleimani, Scott Harris, Rodman Primack, Cynthia Greenawalt, Tonja Adair, Gale St. John, Brian Kornet, Eric Sarver, Joe Putignano, Gus Anderson, Art DeLorenzo, Ivan Drucker, Caroline Green, Bruce Goldfarb, Patrick McHugh, Scott Bloom, Nikki Brotherson, Susann Eaton, Robert Birnbaum, Joshua Newman, Harvey Weissman, Sharon Stein, Allan Pearlman, Charles Pollak, Deborah Sherman, Seline Karakaya, Craig Brown, Harold Alby, Alexa Johnson, Richard Spedale, Matt Perlman, George Grace, Evan Berger, Rich Kiamco, Elizabeth Haag, Matan Koch, Pedro Sanchez, Lisa Dreier, Rafael Flor, John Coonrod, Carol Coonrod, Joan Holmes, Supriya Banavalikar, Anastasia Andrejewski, Leslie Rioux, Vera Bullock, Nadine Cino, Victoria Rowan, Karen Heller, Rosalind Harris, Alayne Faraone, Adrian O'Donnell, Sheela Kangal, Daniel McHenry, Andrew Weltchek, Ghana Leigh, Ana Maria Jomolca, Tom and Beth Warms, Mel Schreiberg, Amber Adams, Zoe Landers, Ruth Kreitzman, Kitty Lee, Dede Redfearn, Carol Christen, Cate Duggar, Vicki Sullivan, Bonnie Harvey, Theresa Boyce, Catherine Curley, Brian London, Tom and Erica Lynch, Michael Burghoffer, Mirra Miller, Mark Simpson, Carolyn Weiss, Paul Weiss (of blessed memory), Robert Jacobson, Louis Brus, Marilyn Brus, Elizabeth Brus, Christina Brus and all those yet to come.

Contents

Preface: Nora Hits Rock Bottom

When I was young, I thought success would be a piece of cake. I was a smart, hard-working student. In fact, I was class president in high school and graduated from an Ivy League university with a high GPA.

But when I got to the work world, all the book smarts and people skills I'd learned in school didn't seem to help me as much as I had thought they would.

I struggled at my first job. When I was doing stuff that I found exciting and interesting, it was easy to do the work. But anything I found boring or tedious would take me 10 times longer than it should have. My boss thought I was really smart, but he was frustrated with my ineffectiveness. "Nora," he would tell me, "I appreciate how well you edit a research paper, but that's not what I hired you to do. I hired you to make travel reservations and manage my Outlook contacts."

But when I made travel reservations and entered business cards, I felt bored and exasperated! I avoided the simplest parts of my job in favor of the much more interesting parts of other people's jobs. Eventually, I started receiving performance reviews saying, "We like you as a person, but you're just no good at your work."

Luckily, I had been building a lot of high-level relationships in my industry while I was avoiding my work. So, just before I was about to be officially fired for incompetence, I got a new job that was much more intellectually challenging. My boss was delighted to support my move and "stay friends." He even offered to sign a recommendation letter that talked about how smart and creative I was as long as I didn't claim to be organized or good at administrative work.

When I arrived at the new job, I knew all my problems were over. The old job had been boring. But the new job was exciting and stimulating.

Everyone there wanted me for my smarts and creativity. I didn't have to do boring stuff anymore. Nothing could go wrong, right?

You can imagine how shocked I was when I started getting bad performance reviews again. But this time, they said, "Although we love your work, on a personal level, you're immature and difficult to work with."

Wait, what? My old boss liked me but not my work. My new bosses liked my work but not me? I think I would have kept struggling like this for many years at different jobs...but fate intervened.

Barely a year into the second job, Hurricane Katrina hit New Orleans, my hometown.

People I grew up with were raped and killed in the Superdome. Some drowned in flood waters. Others died of neglect. The horror of these tragedies triggered waves of pain and grief in me.

I cried daily, on the subway, in the shower, walking down the sidewalk. I had no tools, no strategies, no cute aphorisms that could take the pain away. All I could do was live through the suffering...but barely.

After a few months, I quit my exciting, stimulating job. I thought it would help to get away from work, but I only fell deeper into misery.

Finally, I dragged myself to get help. I started attending support groups, and found gentle listening, kind words and comforting hugs to help heal me. I made new friends and began to put my life back in order.

After a few months of this wonderful support, I took a hard look at my money. My savings were running dangerously low, and I needed to earn money again.

I found a part-time job teaching English as a Second Language. I was just so grateful for the opportunity to earn income. Plus, I got to teach a lovely group of international students. But after a few weeks, I started to see that there were a number of things wrong with the program. It really bugged me. Luckily, I didn't have to worry for long because a few weeks later, I was fired. I decided it was for the best. That company was too dysfunctional for me.

Then I found a job doing light office work for a design firm. This was a much nicer place to work, and I could earn a little more by working more hours. Again, I was grateful for the opportunity. But, within a few weeks, I was bored and annoyed with everything that was wrong about the job. Perhaps the feeling was mutual—they fired me quickly thereafter.

Now I was getting nervous and desperate. My bank account was still very low. But again, I got lucky. A friend introduced me to a recruiter who helped me get a job as a fundraising assistant for a New York City prep school. Finally, a full-time job with enough money to cover my bills doing something interesting.

I was determined to make my new boss happy. And for the first few weeks, I did. But then she went away on vacation. And the projects she left me were soooo boring. She and I agreed they would only take me a few days. But when she returned, she was shocked to find that I hadn't even finished half of the work she had left for me. Plus, new people started right after me, making more money than me, doing more interesting things than me. It made me mad. By Day 70, I was getting warnings. By Day 89, I was fired. Again.

Three jobs in six months. Fired from all of them.

And each time things went south, I thought the problem was outside me:

Pre-Katrina Job #1: Work was too boring.
Pre-Katrina Job #2: They liked my work, but not me.

Post-Katrina Job #3: Program too disorganized.
Post-Katrina Job #4: Annoying boss, annoying colleagues, boring work.
Post-Katrina Job #5: Mean boss, boring work, and other people my age getting promoted into higher-paying, more interesting positions.

But Wait, There Is Good News Too!

The fact that I hit such a low, low, low bottom is what led me to discover the tools that turned my life around. Then I used these tools to help others.

First it was friends in my support groups who wanted to replicate my turnaround.

Then it was senior corporate executives, business owners, whole companies—and before I knew it, I'd helped more than 10,000 people.

I've also worked with more than 100 companies in 40 different industries, so you'll hear me frame the tools from many different perspectives—from the CEO on down to the most junior employees.

I'll reveal the tools shortly.

But just for this moment, let me throw some numbers at you:

- In 2006, the year I got fired from three jobs in six months, I earned $11,000 total.
- In 2007, I saw a 500% increase in my earnings to $55,000.
- In 2008, I more than doubled my earnings to just over $125,000. That was 1000% more than 2006.

I did not make that money teaching these tools (that would come later). I made that money as an employee, working for very human bosses, in a real industry. In other words, long before I started making money by sharing these tools with clients, I was making money by **_USING_** these tools in my own life.

Introduction: Your Brain is Lying to You

I love babies. They're so cuddly and adorable. **And such crazy, weird, android robots!!!**

Paging Captain Kirk!

I'm kidding of course. But only half-kidding.

Did you know that when babies are born, their brains and nerves are the least developed organs in their bodies? What do I mean by that?

Imagine a computer with no programs at all. It may have a fast or slow processor or a large or small hard drive. But it has no software. Now, imagine that this computer acquires software programs only when you type on it. As you type, software programs begin to take shape in the computer. Eventually these programs interact with your typing and get more and more complex. Later on, the computer is filled with all kinds of programs, some you typed directly, some it strung together on its own using things you typed as the building blocks for its own self-generated programs.

A baby's brain and nerves are like that computer. With interactions and experiences, the brain and nerves generate all sorts of ideas, perceptions, and interpretations of the world. The connections that get generated across the brain and between the brain and trillions of nerve cells across the body are what we refer to as the **nervous system.**

The study of the brain and the nervous system is called neuroscience.

I love this word. Neuroscience. Say it with me...

Neuroscience...

OK, now say, Nora-Science.

Get it? Neuroscience...Nora-Science? How could the brain scientists have known that the neuroscience word they made up was such a Nora-friendly word? (Just teasing...maybe.)

So let's talk about this nervous system. In human beings, the nervous system is designed to continue developing AFTER you're born so that your mind and body can learn to defend you from the threats to your survival. In some places, that's running from elephants. In other places, it's running from grizzly bears or forest fires. In other places, it's hiding from saber-toothed tigers.

In Search of Saber-Toothed Tigers

What? You haven't seen any saber-toothed tigers lately? That's funny. Because your nervous system has been looking for them since you were a baby.

Why?

Because survival is so, so, so important, your nervous system is way more interested in the threats to your survival than in anything else. That's why it's often so much easier to remember the negative, painful, traumatic experiences of our lives than the humdrum ones or the nice-enough ones.

Childhood Survival Skills Don't Work in the Work World

In ancient times, your nervous system's job was to gather information for your adult survival throughout your childhood. If you grew up facing threats from stampeding elephants, then you faced stampeding elephants in adulthood as well. Same goes for saber-toothed tigers and grizzly bears.

But here in the modern world, the threats you grow up defending against are **completely different** from the issues you face in the work world. The skills you learned to survive in childhood will sometimes work for you and other times work against you in the world of work.

The Childhood/Work Connection

Any time someone is struggling at work, my first question is about their parents and their childhood.

Danielle's Story: "Why are you always taking so much?"

Danielle was a talented musician and composer. Born on the Upper East Side of Manhattan to wealthy parents, she lived in a large city in Eastern Canada, though she traveled the world performing at high-profile events and debuting impressive classical works with orchestras on multiple continents.

I met her through friends years before we worked together, and I always marveled at her illustrious career. When she asked to schedule a coaching session with me, I was surprised to find out why. It turned out that Danielle was desperate for income. She had lived for years off of a family inheritance. If she continued operating at her current rate, she would run out of money in a few short months.

Naturally, I asked about her prestigious touring schedule. It turned out that she had not been paid for a commission, a new piece or a performance for many years. I have known and worked with a large number of other musicians. I know that many people earn a good living doing what Danielle does (and doing a lot less than what Danielle does).

"People think I have this amazing career," she told me. "But I haven't earned money in so long." Her face was red with shame.

I spoke slowly and gently as I inquired, "Danielle, is it all right for me to ask you some questions?" She nodded as tears began to run down her cheeks.

Our conversation began with questions about how her parents related to money. Her mother had been stingy and angry whenever Danielle needed money as a pre-teen and young adult. Her father had been anxious and worried whenever she asked for anything. "I remember I went to my father for money for a field trip—it would have been just a few dollars. But it took him an hour to give it to me," she told me.

It's important to let my clients know that they're not alone, to share little pieces of my own history. I want to create an experience for them so they feel I'm kneeling beside them in the universal human journey of grief and healing.

"My mother got really angry whenever I asked for money as a child," I told her. "My father was super anxious and always worried when it was time to pay for stuff."

"It sounds like we had the same parents." She cracked half a smile.

"My mother was weird about a lot of other things too," I told her, "she would watch me like a hawk around food. She was always criticizing my body, telling me I was fat, ugly, disgusting, an embarrassment to her in public. She put me on my first diet when I was six. I don't remember a time in childhood when I wasn't either obsessively dieting or secretly binging. The shame and deprivation were constant."

"Oh my goodness! My mother was obsessed with food. She hated when I ate. She would get so upset when she saw me eating. I was such a tiny child, very slim, but every time she saw me serve food to myself on a plate, she would harangue me for it. It was always 'Why are you always taking so much.'" Her eyes widened as she imitated her mother, "'WHY ARE YOU ALWAYS TAKING SO MUCH?' It was like she wanted me to go hungry."

"How did that make you feel, Danielle?"

"I tried to make myself invisible. I wanted nothing more than to be safe and far away from my mother."

I switched gears..."Danielle, do you ever have the chance to request payment for all these concerts and commissioned works you do?"

"I do, Nora, but it's always the same. When it's time to ask for money, I go mute. I collapse. I can barely breathe."

Danielle's extreme response betrayed more than the frustration of waiting an hour for her father to fish a few bills out of his wallet. Her internal distress came from a much earlier pattern in childhood. A pattern that equated nourishment and deprivation with life and death.

I believe that Danielle's pattern of feeling unworthy of resources began when her mother withheld food and shamed her for the most basic human expression of need: hunger. Those patterns were reinforced as Danielle grew and needed more than food—money, clothes, attention, love, support. Danielle's mother punished her whenever she expressed a need of any kind. Money came later in childhood, but it fell neatly into the terrifying pattern of being deprived of life-giving resources and shamed for needing them.

Tool: Find Your Childhood Money Messages

Now that you know a little more about Danielle and me, I hope you can see that you're not alone. If you want to break through your money and work issues, it's time to ask yourself...

How did my mom talk to me about money, about food, about meeting my needs?

What did I decide about myself, my mom, about money, food, love, about my needs?

How did my dad talk to me about money, about food, about meeting my needs?

What did I decide about myself, my dad, about money, food, love, about my needs?

How have I carried these messages into my work life?

How have I carried these messages into my view of myself at work?

How have I carried these messages into my willingness to voice my opinion, to listen to others, to accept the differences between people?

How have I carried these messages into my willingness to take healthy risks at work, try new things, learn, grow and listen to feedback?

How have I carried these messages into my interactions with people at work? At home? In other areas of life?

The 9 Lies Holding You Back

The 9 Lies Holding You Back are all connected to messages you received as a child that your nervous system translated into self-protection and survival mechanisms. I know they don't always feel like protection mechanisms. Sometimes they just feel like great big blocks. But I promise, we are going to blast through them and here they are…

Lie #1: If They Changed, Everything Would Be OK

Lie #2: Maybe I'm No Good

Lie #3: Work Can't Be Fun

Lie #4: If I'm Procrastinating, Something Is Wrong

Lie #5: My Boss Is Crazy

Lie #6: I Have to Be Perfect to Succeed

Lie #7: I Can't Ask for What I Want

Lie #8: The Problem Is the Economy

Lie #9: If I Succeed, Others Will Fail

So Many Lies!!

Wow. There are so many ways our nervous systems lie to us about our work life. Now, I want you to consider an alternative reality. What if you could enjoy your work, earn well, feel good about your colleagues and clients, feel good about yourself, feel good about your personal life and your work/life balance…and just have an all-around great time? Well, then, it's time to blast through these 9 Lies.

Lie #1: If They Changed, Everything Would Be OK

This lie is the most important lie for us to blast through. Without it, we can't really do anything else.

Have you ever heard someone say, "Stop making me feel so guilty!" or "Honey, you make me so happy" or "You broke my heart"?

I would hope so. This is how people talk.

It's also how all of us express ourselves when our nervous systems are telling their MOST IMPORTANT lie.

Biologically, there's only one place thoughts, feelings and sensations come from. They come from INSIDE the body that's feeling them. And yet, your brain is programmed to tell you that your feelings come from things happening outside you. In other words, you project what you feel inside as coming from things that are outside you. That seems odd, doesn't it?

Actually it's kind of awesome. Here's why:

It's a very bad idea to pause in thought when facing a saber-toothed tiger.

Asking yourself deep probing questions about the nature of reality and perception will probably result in your becoming a tasty breakfast for that big scary cat.

So even though you may not see any saber-toothed tigers this week, if your nervous system is telling you that you're in a situation right now that is making you angry and upset, then you're probably reacting with the same brain cells that would do a great job protecting you from that saber-toothed tiger.

The problem is that, in a moment of fear, those brain cells are telling you that what you see is as real and threatening as a saber-toothed tiger, even though it probably isn't. More lies!! Yikes!!

Now, I'm not saying that there aren't some other people who can be really difficult to deal with.

Believe me, I've known some difficult people. Oof! I get a yucky feeling in my stomach just thinking about some of those folks.

But even if people are super difficult or super crazy, as long as we see them as the problem, we are allowing our nervous system to shut off our opportunities for growth.

So, in addition to all the ways they annoy us, it turns out these difficult people are also blocking our personal growth? Talk about unfair!!

So, are you ready to take your growth back?

Awesome!

Here is the first step: LOOK FOR THE PAIN...

A Nora Story: Pain Is the Ticket to Get on the Train

Because of all the support groups I joined after Katrina, I had friends to talk to when I got fired from each of those three post-Katrina jobs. Kind, experienced, loving friends who had seen a whole lot more than the folks I kept in touch with from high school and college. These were mentors who could affirm my worth and value while gently encouraging me to focus on my own behavior rather than all the problems "out there" that led to my frustrations.

But I could only see a limited part of my role. I was blinded by my frustration with other people and outside circumstances.

What did it take for me to focus my attention on myself?

I wish I could tell you that it was some white light moment or spiritual transformation. But the answer is far more humdrum.

What it took was pain—searing, miserable, garden variety pain. When I got fired for the third time in six months, the pain was worse than it had ever been. Finally, I had received the Gift Of Desperation (and yes, those words spell G-O-D).

Because it was only with the Gift Of Desperation that I was finally able to listen to Good Orderly Direction (Look, it's G-O-D, again!).

I called and called and called and called people. I asked for help and cried and asked for guidance and cried and asked for help and cried.

And I cried.

Did I mention that I cried?

"Pain is the ticket to get on the train," my friends told me.

"This better be a freaking amazing train," I would reply.

With the willingness that comes from pain, I was able to look back at my checkered job history and see that...

I was the one at the scene of the crime.

And not just one crime...every crime...reaching far back into post-graduation temp jobs, college work-study, and part-time high school jobs. In fact, every time money was involved, things had started out pretty great and then gone south...***FAST.***

Tool: Find Your Train Ticket

So, where is YOUR pain?

Are you unhappy at work?

Have you recently lost a job?

Are you struggling with a boss?

Are you annoyed with a co-worker or several co-workers?

Do you feel overwhelmed by the weird people dynamics at work? (Some people call this "workplace politics.")

Congratulations! This frustrating, annoying struggle you're having is your ticket to get on the growth train!

I know, I know. This better be a freaking amazing train.

I think you'll find that it is. Ready? All aboard!

Finding Your Saber-Toothed Tiger

Why am I so excited that you have your train ticket right now? Translation: Why am I so excited that you've identified the things that are causing you pain and discomfort? Because if these people or situations are upsetting you, then I promise you that your nervous system has told you in some way, shape or form that if those people or situations changed, your life would be better. That's the lie, right?

So what's the new reality?

The new reality I'd like to offer you is that every time someone does something you don't like, you have an incredible opportunity to:

- Reach out for the love and support you deserve.
- Bond with your fellow human beings over the common experience of pain, frustration and discomfort.
- Identify skills that will help you deal with the situation, take good care of yourself, and expand your capacity to be useful to others.
- Practice those skills.
- *And get so good at those skills that when ANOTHER disturbing situation happens (and life is filled with difficult situations), you'll handle it with an aptitude and poise that will continue to support your growth and bring value to others.*

But you know what I love most about this new reality?

It's a reality where you take the focus OFF changing other people's behavior (since they are WAAAAAAAY outside your control) and you put the focus on your OWN feelings and behaviors.

Is it easy to change our own perceptions, feelings and behaviors? Sometimes it's very easy. Sometimes, it's SO HARD!! Often, it's sort of a combination. But changing ourselves is definitely possible. And that's more than I can say for changing other people.

Building a Tribe for Safety

So, if you use pain as an opportunity to grow and change your own behavior, then all your problems will be solved, right?

You've probably heard that focusing on your own behavior is the path to growth.

So why haven't you already done it? Why isn't your life perfect yet?

Of course you know I'm teasing, but have you ever noticed that no matter how well we know these good, wise ideas, we still struggle when stuff really doesn't go our way?

Here's what I think is really going on:

When things don't go your way, your nervous system throws you into survival defense mode—as if you are face to face with a saber-toothed tiger all by yourself in the forest...and it's either fight, run, or be breakfast!!!

This survival defense mode is so much more powerful than your smart, wise thoughts about personal growth because your survival defense mode has been keeping you and your ancestors alive for thousands of years.

Humans needed to be able to spring into defense mode long before they needed to read, write, or pontificate about the best life philosophies.

So, if your survival mode is going to keep outrunning your smartest, best thinking, how on earth can I help you change your behavior?

How about I give your survival mode what it needs to feel safe and sound, even in the scariest, most uncomfortable situations in your life? This way, you can feel **SAFE** enough to slow down, think differently, act differently and achieve all kinds of new results.

So, in order to get different outcomes around the things that make you feel the **MOST UNSAFE**, I have to find a way to help you feel **SUPER-SAFE.**

To do that, I'll help you do what our ancestors who lived in the wilderness did.

Converting Anger-Defense (Fight) to Safety

Imagine that you're all alone in the forest and suddenly a big scary bear starts charging at you. You'll be pretty jumpy and terrified, trying to fight that big scary bear like your life depends on it UNTIL a bunch of warriors from your tribe come running. Now, you're calm, confident and ready to fight off the bear as a group.

Converting Fear-Defense (Flight) to Safety

Now imagine that you're running from a forest fire and there's nowhere to hide. Everywhere you look, trees are engulfed in flames. You'll feel pretty desperate and hopeless UNTIL you hear voices calling you to a nearby cave where a bunch of men and women from your tribe have found shelter to protect themselves and you from the fire.

Converting Rejection-Defense (Shame) to Safety

Now imagine that you've accidentally violated some ancient tribal taboo and tribal law says that you have to be cast out alone into the wilderness (where you will surely die). You'll feel pretty consumed with shame and fear UNTIL several tribal elders come to your defense and demand that you be allowed to stay since it was an honest mistake.

Did you see a common theme in these three examples? Yup, that theme is tribal support. One friend is lovely. A few friends are great. But it takes a tribe of support to create the feeling of safety that will soothe your nervous system out of defensive survival mode and into healthy learning and growing mode.

In fact, I believe that building a tribe will give you the love, support and COURAGE it takes to see past the automatic defenses of your childhood programming, and put the focus on yourself in ways that allow you to heal old wounds, discover all kinds of new skills, and develop your capacity to achieve growth beyond what you imagine is possible.

So let's build that tribe...

Dahlia's Story: "I get to have friends outside of work?"

Dahlia was a young, dynamic tech entrepreneur who had developed a super cool new app. Her app had become so popular and successful that investors had approached her about expanding her company to help her launch more apps and increase market share.

But within a few months of the investment, Dahlia began to act strangely. She started yelling and crying a lot. And she was suddenly unable to complete work within deadlines, if at all.

Her employees had begun to fear her, and her investors were worried for her sanity.

When she and I began working together, I immediately asked about the people she connected with outside her company. "What do you mean, outside the company?" she asked. "There's life outside the company?"

Slowly she began to tell me about how isolated, terrified and overwhelmed she'd become. "I created this company out of love because I loved the idea for my app. But now, there's no love for me in the company, and it's making me miserable!"

"Dahlia," I said, "you deserve love. And you deserve to love what you do. But you can't expect emotional support and love from the people you work with, especially when you're the boss."

"So where do I get it?" She was nearly in tears.

"We all need a tribe," I began, "but the tribe that will keep you safe and supported is a tribe outside work, not inside work. You can have great relationships at work. You can collaborate and brainstorm and achieve together in the best ways. But you need to be able to work through your own nervous system defenses outside work with safe, loving, nurturing friends so that you can bring your best, most peaceful self to the work environment."

"I think that makes sense," said Dahlia, "but why does it make me feel so bad to think about?"

And then we began to talk about Dahlia's family. It was a painful story—a difficult, angry, withholding father; a gentle, loving mother who was too afraid to stand up to her father.

"When we come from difficult childhoods, it's really normal to look around adulthood for the family we always wished we had when we were kids. It's especially common for us to look for that family in the workplace. The problem is that we just can't get the family-level healing and nurturing we crave from work colleagues AND be superstar workers at the same time.

"It's beautiful and healthy that you still crave the love and safety you missed out on in childhood. But you'll be so much happier if you build yourself a tribe OUTSIDE of work. That way, you will strengthen your inner resources so much that work becomes a place of giving and service rather than a place of deprivation and misery."

So Dahlia got to work—outside of work. She called old friends. She made new ones. She began checking in with different friends each day. She began making dates with buddies just to talk and catch up. They talked about work. They talked about other stuff.

And within a few weeks, she was singing a different tune: "Wow, Nora, who knew that having a life outside my job would make me better at my job?" And it was true. Dahlia was calmer, warmer and more connected to everyone she worked with because she was getting what she needed from her tribe.

Building a Tribe

I look back now and feel SO LUCKY to have gone through the horrible pain and grief I experienced after Hurricane Katrina. I'm certain this pain is what drove me to join many support groups.

More importantly, though, I didn't just attend the group meetings, I connected with individual people by phone and in person, day in and day out.

As those individual connections grew into friendships, I realized that, until Katrina, I had always looked to a small number of close friends to support me when I needed it. But when those folks fell short (as all humans do some of the time), I felt hollow and lonely.

By seeking to connect with a circle of supporters, I was not relying on the availability of one person or even a few people. Once I had a big enough tribe, I saw that as long as I was willing to make a few more phone calls, I would eventually reach someone and get the support I needed. Very quickly, I got the chance to practice both giving and receiving support. This made me feel useful and valuable in a really special way.

I met all sorts of people in these support groups, but I gravitated toward a very particular set of qualities in people. At first, I simply marveled that this set of qualities existed. Then, slowly I learned to start imitating these qualities...very, very slowly.

What qualities did my new friends have?

- They were kind and compassionate.

- They knew that they didn't know what was best for me (or for themselves).

- They were willing to discover answers to their own problems with patience and open-heartedness.

- They didn't try to tell me what to do unless I asked for their advice.

- They understood that pain is part of growth.

- They didn't try to make my pain go away when I shared it. But they did listen with love and understanding.

- They celebrated my joy and victories with me. They had true generosity of spirit.

Tool: Build Your Tribe

Whom in your life do you feel safe with?

Are they part of your tribe? If not, would you like them to be?

Whom in your life do you feel inspired by?

Are they part of your tribe? If not, would you like them to be?

Creating Tribal Relationships

If you're looking to expand your tribe, here's how:

Make a list of about 20 people you like.

Call, text, email or connect with each one about 1-2 times per week for six weeks.

When you reach them, start by making sure you've reached them at a good time.

If you have, tell them something nice but not suffocating ("I was just thinking about you and how sweet you are" or "I was just thinking about how smart that idea of yours was last week").

Then ask about their day, their life, what's cooking with them.

If there's still time, share a little about you: positive news to share, uncertainties on your mind, feelings coming up in positive and negative ways.

If you just practice reaching out to people you like on a regular (but not stalker) basis, I promise some of them will become members of your close, intimate tribe.

Can you control who does and who doesn't? NOPE.

All you can do is keep showing up, reaching out, connecting and letting the process naturally take its course. This is the way friendships get built. If you only call people one, two or three times a week, after a few weeks, you'll notice who's coming closer and who's not. Go where it's warm!

Vulnerability is POWER. Feeling safe enough to process your feelings with safe people is the first step toward unhooking from your nervous system's defenses against the imaginary saber-toothed tigers in your life, especially at work.

Building our tribe consistently is essential to creating the ongoing safety necessary to begin the one set of changes we are capable of—changing ourselves.

Changing ourselves for the better can be scary and painful! Yikes! But with wonderful people to listen to our natural, healthy feelings of uncomfortable growth and to cheer us on, we'll actually have the safety and support we deserve that will give us the courage to GROW out of our comfort zone perceptions and into a whole new reality of success.

Putting the Focus on Ourselves

So once I had been loved and comforted around the pain of losing three jobs in six months, the Good Orderly Direction that I got again and again was to put the focus on myself.

What does that mean? It means that when I looked at the painful situation of being fired so many times, even though my head wanted me to blame other people and circumstances for my pain, I asked my friends to give me the love and support I needed so that I could feel safe enough to look at my own behavior.

Here's what I found:

First, I began to admit to myself that I had struggled in a lot of jobs. In fact, when I looked back, I realized I was reprimanded or threatened with being fired at every job I'd ever had.

Second, I began to admit to myself what the nature of that struggle really came down to:

I didn't want to do what I was supposed to do.

It was strange. I wasn't consumed with angry, rebellious thoughts. I didn't have a bone to pick with "the man." I didn't think my bosses were trying to screw me over.

Does it sound too simple to say that I had a really hard time following directions?

But luckily, the world has been talking about the way childhood colors adulthood for a very long time. And I was lucky enough to have friends who encouraged me to think about childhood experiences that may have influenced this seemingly strange resistance to following directions.

And when I did...

I grew up in a home with very few clear directions, healthy rules or safe boundaries. My parents divorced when I was four and my dad dropped out of the picture emotionally—though he was still around to fight with my mom about money neither one of them had.

By the time I turned five, my mother was crying on my shoulder and leaning on me for emotional support. Something in me figured out how to perform at giving her what she needed—how to follow the most important unspoken and terrifying rule in the house: Make sure Mommy is OK.

I spent years resenting my mother for all the time I spent taking care of her from age five on into my college years. But I don't anymore. Now, I can see what a terrified young woman she was—a single mother with two children, a difficult relationship with her ex-husband, and very, very little money. It must have been incredibly hard. It was a courageous act to raise two kids while struggling at work, at home, with her angry ex (my dad), and with her own terrible pain from her own severely abusive childhood.

As courageous as she was, my mother never had the tribe of loving support that she deserved. I believe everyone deserves nurturing people to cheer them on as they take risks and face pain. My mom didn't know she deserved it and didn't know how to ask the right people for it.

So, she leaned on me. And she gave me some messages that were confusing to a little girl.

There were a lot of unclear expectations, a lot of anger at the world, at my father, at me—for not reading her mind...for not figuring out what she needed and giving it to her...for a lot of things.

She yelled a lot and frequently flew into explosive rages. In fact, my earliest memory of life is of seeing her punch my father. As a tiny, vulnerable child, I was terrified of her physically and felt unsafe around her.

She never gave me a bedtime or taught me how to clean my room or organize my desk. There were not many gentle, loving clear directions.

It became clear to me at an early age that figuring out how to please her was essential to my physical survival. But following step-by-step directions was not.

And so, once in a while, when she asked me to do simple things like set the table or help with dinner—things that weren't hard for me to figure out how to do—I resisted. It was a subtle way to sabotage her power over me, to act out the anger that was far too unsafe to communicate directly for fear of her explosive rage.

It was easy for me to have a deep sense of oppression and unexpressed rage at feeling so unsafe around my mother—at being better at figuring out and meeting her needs than she was at meeting mine.

And it turned out that this same rage had followed me into every set of instructions I was supposed to follow in every job I had ever had. Is it any wonder I got fired so many times? I couldn't do what anyone asked me to do!

Tool: Put the Focus on Yourself

What behavior do you think **you** might be doing that could be contributing to your problems?

If you're unhappy at work, are you bringing a negative attitude to work each day?

If you're feeling underpaid, are you resisting asking for a raise?

If you've been denied a raise, are you procrastinating on looking for higher-paying work?

If you recently lost your job, are you afraid to look at the ways you may have been ineffective with tasks or with people?

If you're struggling with a boss, do you feel that looking at your own behavior will mean that he or she is right to criticize or abuse you? (It won't ever, ever mean that.)

If you're searching for a better paying job, are you selling yourself short?

Are you willing to lean hard on your tribe as you ask yourself these questions? Remember, growing past your current status will feel nearly impossible if you don't have oodles of support for the feelings that will come up.

If you don't have that support, your nervous system will go right back to telling you that your feelings are coming from outside you and you have to fight, fly and lie in order to be safe.

I can tell you not to believe your nervous system till I'm blue in the face, but if you don't have real live humans giving you love, support and a listening ear, your nervous system will just tell you that I'm crazy and all your problems are over there.

Do you want to believe that all your problems are coming from over there? Or do you want to unleash your career success? You can't have both. (Sorry, I wish I could make it easier for you.)

If you choose to be unleash your success, then READ ON!

And if you choose to keep believing that other people are the problem, I will still think you are lovable and valuable. It will just be hard to use the rest of the tools in this book.

So...which one do you choose?

Lie #2: Maybe I'm NO GOOD

Isn't it funny how quickly we go from blaming others to blaming ourselves?

I am not asking you to blame yourself.

When we "put the focus on ourselves," it's to discover opportunities to expand our capacities, NOT to blame or shame ourselves.

But remember, your nervous system thinks that uncomfortable feelings are the enemy. If I convince your nervous system that you are the source of your uncomfortable feelings, it could be really easy to assume that YOU are the saber-toothed tiger and then it might start fighting you. So, if you had any feelings of low self-esteem or you noticed yourself beating yourself up as you read the last chapter, congratulations! You're a human being with a very survival-focused nervous system! And nervous systems beat up the humans they live in if those humans aren't receiving both love and wisdom as they grow.

And even THEN, our nervous systems still beat us up a little and blame others too. Even when we're really on the super-growth track.

So am I saying that your nervous system is programmed to hate you AND everyone else around you? Well, in survival mode, sometimes, yes.

You see, part of what I want to teach you is how to be loving to yourself and others as you grow.

Jim's Story: Don't Be Stupid

Jim was a car salesman in a major California city. I know what you're thinking. A car salesman! Really? It's true. A car salesman. And the only person who hated car salesmen more than you or anyone you know was Jim.

You see, Jim had one of the strongest commitments to integrity that I have ever seen. His father had died in a car accident when he was a teenager and, after that, he became obsessed with helping people buy cars that would keep them safe and well. He was one of the most knowledgeable people about driver safety, consumer preference and ownership satisfaction surveys that I have ever met.

But Jim was struggling at work. He'd been the hardest worker at his dealership for more years than he cared to admit but his sales numbers were still in the bottom half of his region.

When we began our work together, he told me that after all the research he'd done on vehicle safety and car owner satisfaction, he was 100% sure that he had the capacity to identify the car that was exactly right for anyone who walked into the dealership. He would listen to their needs for a while and then walk them over to his choice and explain why it was **perfect** for them. If they balked, he would show them elaborate research pertaining to accident fatalities, satisfaction surveys and relevant demographics. If he had to, he would show them every number under the sun to prove how safe and happy they would be in this car.

But, it was shocking to him that about 75% of them walked away. He would become even more annoyed when he found out that many of those same customers ended up going to other dealerships and buying cars that were often much more dangerous, and a very bad fit for their actual needs.

Naturally, I was curious about his childhood. He told me that his father had been a man of impeccable integrity who always took responsibility for his actions and trained his four sons to do the same.

Jim seemed to idolize his father. He talked about him as a pillar of their community, going to work every day with no complaints, totally committed to supporting his family and to being a good husband and father. No one ever yelled in Jim's home. No one ever hit anyone else.

But there was something that didn't quite sit right with me as Jim shared his childhood recollections.

Finally, after a few sessions, I began to understand. Jim believed that his father was committed to teaching him to approach life with the same strong sense of integrity and personal responsibility that he himself had.

To do that, whenever Jim had a problem as a kid, his father had refused to allow him to complain and instead insisted that Jim look at where he was being stupid or irresponsible.

"Where are you being stupid, Jim? Don't be stupid. Use your head. Do what's right."

One time when a neighborhood bully beat young Jim to a pulp, his father refused to comfort him or allow him to cry. Instead, he drove Jim over to the bully's house. Jim was quaking with fear but Jim's father insisted that Jim face the bully down.

It was a story Jim told with a mixture of pride and sadness. Over several sessions, we explored the implications of the story. Jim decided he could appreciate that his father had helped him learn to face his fear. But he also felt a sense of sorrow for the terrified child he had been and the lack of empathy his father had shown for his feelings.

Jim felt guilty for saying or thinking anything negative about his father. So I offered Jim an alternate interpretation. "Jim," I said, "I think it's great to appreciate how much your father was committed to your success in life. But perhaps, your Dad didn't realize how much of a black/white, right/wrong perspective he unintentionally imparted to you. After all, any time things didn't go your way, there had to be someone to blame—either you or someone else."

"So you're saying that even though my Dad never told me to have this rigid point of view, somehow my childhood brain interpreted my father's words and actions to mean that anytime things don't go my way, I have blame to myself or others."

"Pretty much."

At the car dealership, this blame thing wasn't working for Jim. He either felt terrible about his failure to serve his potential customers or he felt terrible for thinking his customers were stupid. Either way, Jim's conviction that his lack of success meant he deserved blame, shame, and guilt was the primary block to Jim's growth.

Crafty, Creeping Blame and Shame

Blame is such a cunning phenomenon. Whether your parents taught you to blame yourself or blame others, as soon as blame is on the table, it's not long before we feel pretty terrible about ourselves.

And then you're stuck in a blame cycle.

All it takes is a sense of judgment or shame about things going "wrong." That judgment can be for other people. That shame can be for yourself. Usually, it's a little of both.

When I first told Jim, "You know, those people who decide not to buy from you, they're not wrong or stupid," he got rather offended.

"Are you saying I'm wrong and stupid then? Even though I have the statistics and studies that prove how much happier and safer they'll be with the car I've picked out for them?"

"Nope, you're not wrong or stupid."

"Well, one of us has to be wrong."

"Actually, no. Neither of you has to be wrong. But as long as you believe that one of you has to be wrong if they don't agree with you, then it's going to be very painful to talk to people no matter what they think about you or their cars."

"Well, what else is there?"

"Well, I believe that we're all tiny humans perceiving an incomprehensibly giant world. So if that's true, what if nobody has the market cornered on right and wrong? What if all we can do is learn a little bit from one another? And what if the only thing to do when things don't work out the way we expect is to look for the blind spot we may not have realized was there before?"

"Aren't blind spots just moments when you're wrong and stupid?" Jim was having a hard time letting go of the right/wrong model. But it was understandable. He'd been using it for many decades.

"I don't see blind spots as times of stupidity or judgment or shame," I said. "I see blind spots as opportunities for expanding our tiny human perceptions with gentleness and courage."

This short-circuited Jim's head a little. Gentleness and courage in his mind were as different as pillows and hammers. And he said as much.

"Jim, I know that pain and fear can be great motivators for growth. But I don't believe that the best, most consistent growth can ever come from constant fear and pain. My own journey and my experiences with thousands of others have shown me that pain and fear are mixed into many moments of trying anything new. BUT if we don't have enough love and gentleness to help us through the pain of confronting our blind spots and discovering new opportunities for growth, we'll fall too quickly into shame, blame, and judgment and we'll never have the inner strength to take action."

"You see, Jim, I believe wisdom and intelligence can help guide us to new information, but without compassion, support and gentleness from others, we'll never have the courage to take new action. And courage isn't about smarts. It's about feeling fear with an open heart but taking action anyway. In fact, the word courage is literally derived from the French word for heart."

Are You Like Jim?

Are you blaming either yourself or others when things don't go your way?

What would it feel like to view others as tiny imperfect humans in a vast unknowable world?

What would it feel like to be gentle and kind to yourself as a tiny, imperfect human in a vast unknowable world, especially when things don't go your way?

What if reaching out for loving support that cheers you on for feeling your feelings AND taking action was the best way to give yourself the courage to face new growth?

What if you could give and receive love and acceptance as you look for your own blind spots and opportunities for growth?

Jim's Transformation...

Over several sessions, Jim and I talked through the right/wrong paradigm his parents had given him. Eventually, he began to recognize that he was so busy trying to make customers see that he was right, that he forgot to help them feel comfortable.

In fact, because he was so focused on proving the "rightness" of his perspectives to customers, Jim often unknowingly made his customers feel wrong and unsafe. When they felt wrong and unsafe, they went to someone else to buy their cars.

But once Jim shifted his focus from right/wrong and blame/shame to gentle listening and focusing on creating comfort and safety, his sales began to climb.

Because Jim still loved collecting great information, he often had information to share that was more useful than most of the other car salesmen he knew. But now, he only delivered it in a context of valuing connection and safety over right or wrong data.

Within six months, Jim became the #1 Salesman at his dealership.

A Nora Story: The Courage to Change

After I was fired from three jobs in six months in 2006, I was finally desperate enough to stop blaming other people and start focusing on myself. But focusing on myself was scary!!

What if I was wrong, bad, stupid, incompetent, or not good enough? I called my friends to talk about it. They were so supportive.

"That's great, Nora!"

"You're so brave to look at yourself so honestly!"

"I hear a lot of humility in what you're saying and it's really inspiring."

"I love hearing you letting go of blame and resentment and really finding the courage to look at yourself. That's very scary stuff, my dear. Good work!"

I so badly needed to hear this reinforcement from such kind people.

In my house growing up, whenever my parents struggled at work (and they both struggled at work), it was either someone else's fault or they beat themselves up.

My mom came home crying because a man from another department at her job had been mean to her. But she made herself feel worse when she lambasted herself for not "handling him better." Unfortunately, getting angry at herself didn't seem to help her handle him better at all.

Sometimes, when my mom got upset about work, I was the problem. She got angry with me for interrupting her at work if I needed something, or if I called her to pick me up from school because I missed the bus. I remember feeling so lonely as I sat alone, late in the day, on the steps of the school for more than an hour. Then, when she arrived to pick me up, she yelled at me for taking her away from her job.

My dad got fired because he was late again and again and again...but he was annoyed that his bosses didn't understand how bad traffic was. AND, he told me years later that he was filled with negative feelings about himself that were so bad that he would do anything to distract himself from those feelings. This distraction became so compulsive that it was as though he lived his whole life in procrastination.

I don't remember my father expressing anger at himself the way my mother expressed anger towards herself. And yet, somehow I learned to be just like him with distraction and procrastination. I continue to be amazed by the ways we imitate our parents.

My mom complained and complained about her boss. He was so rude. He was so egotistical. He was always doing it TO her. He was always making her feel trapped and hopeless and down on herself.

Following in my parents' footsteps, I had felt trapped and hopeless whenever something didn't go my way at any job. It wasn't that this was how I wanted to think. It was the ONLY way I knew how to think about work. I didn't know any other alternatives. Nothing else was programmed into my nervous system. My childhood experiences simply told me that if something was wrong, it was either someone else's fault or my fault.

In adulthood, work was a lose-lose situation for me. I felt negative feelings toward myself and others no matter where I worked. No wonder I had been fired so many times.

But here I was, talking to my tribe, seeking to find flaws in my behavior without beating up on myself. And it was **amazing** to talk with these people who told me I was brave, BRAVE!

Brave to stop blaming my problems on other people.

Brave to look for my own shortcomings with gentleness.

Brave to find out which of my behaviors kept me from being a great employee.

Brave to search for things about myself that I could actually change with help, guidance, and support.

It didn't sound like it would be terribly easy to change myself, but my friends helped me see that changing myself was a lot more likely than changing anyone else.

Breaking Through Blame

Were you like me?

Did you watch your parents blame their problems on other people?

Did you hear your parents complain about the economy, the industry, their bosses, their colleagues, the fact that life just isn't fair?

Did you hear your parents blame their problems on you?

Did you hear your parents blame *your* problems on you?

Do you find yourself taking things personally at work?

Do you find that your feelings get hurt very easily when people offer criticism at work or in life?

Can you give yourself permission to be gentle with yourself and others?

Can you give yourself permission to be a human being who will always make mistakes and have flaws?

Can you give yourself permission to accept that you will never be able to see the full picture of the vast world or even a many-sided situation through your very tiny human perceptions?

Tool: Expand Your Tribe

I believe there are words we need to hear again and again and again. These words give us the courage and strength to keep facing the ups and downs of life as we seek to grow. And these words, whatever they may be for each of us, always come with listening, gentleness and kindness.

You want people in your tribe who are kind, supportive and gentle. And the only way to find those people is to **be a person who says kind, supportive, gentle words to other people.** So let's practice:

Make a list of five people you like. Try calling or texting each one of them with a gentle check-in message or question.

The message can be something like: "Hope you're having a great day!" or "I was thinking about you today. I'm sending good vibes your way!"

The question could be: "How's your day going? Anything you'd like to share?"

If and when you actually chat on the phone, practice asking them how they are, how things are at work, at home, etc.

NOW, HERE'S THE KICKER:

When they answer your question, practice saying the things like:

"You're not alone."
"I'm with you."
"I'm kneeling beside you."
"I hear you."
"You're being so brave to be so honest about your feelings!"
"You're being so brave to be so honest about where your defenses might be stopping you!"
"You're being so brave to let go of judgment of others and instead focus on what you can discover about yourself!"
"You're being so brave to look for your own personal growth!"

"That sounds really hard, I'm sorry."
"That sounds really great, I'm so happy for you!"

These words work because they're not advice. They're just support. And I think you'd rather have people support you than fix you. So perhaps others feel the same way?

The Compassion of a Friend

There is a story I've heard many times that always makes me cry. Thinking of it now, I'm tearing up as I start to type.

There's a man walking down a street and he falls into a big hole.

He looks frantically for a way out but he can't find one. Finally, he begins to call out to passers-by for help.

As he looks up, he sees a doctor in his white lab coat and calls out to him, "Doctor, Doctor, please help me! I've fallen into this hole."

The doctor strides over to him and says, "I see that you have. Let me write you this prescription to make it better." Then he takes out his prescription pad, writes a prescription and drops it into the hole, before walking away.

Then the man sees a priest walking by. "Father, Father, help me please! I've fallen into this hole!"

"Oh, what a troubling turn of events, my son. Here, let me give you this prayer to comfort you in your hour of need." Then the priest takes out a prayer card and drops it into the hole, before walking away.

Finally, the man sees a friend walking by, "Buddy, buddy, hey buddy! Can you help me? I've fallen into this hole!"

His buddy walks up to the edge of the hole and then jumps in with his friend.

Now the man is exasperated. "What did you do that for? Now we're both trapped!"

His friend smiles at him and says, "Well I fell into this hole last week and I know the way out. Come on, let me show you."

The Pain of Growth

Gaining insight into ourselves can be painful. The nervous system uses blame and judgment as a defense against that pain. Releasing blame and judgment can open up a deep sense of grief as we discover the wounds and fears of childhood that lie beneath our defenses. In my journey, I was fortunate to have plenty of people who could identify with me as I lived through the vulnerable feelings hiding under the tough defenses.

We all need and deserve love and support as we release defenses. Old wounds open up, and we begin to listen to the terrified little kids inside us who used those defenses to survive all those years ago. Building a tribe of loving, nurturing friends is the fast track to new actions that will change your work life.

Lie #3: Work Can't Be Fun

Many, many people grow up thinking that work has to be hard, challenging, painful, effortful, virtuous and miserable. After all, it's work, not play, right?

Emmanuel's Story: We're Allowed to Do That?

Emmanuel and his small team of seven people ran a graphic design firm that did amazing work: graphics, logos, and branding for some of the most important companies in the country. It was remarkable to see them do their creative work. They were a little bit like graphics rock stars.

But since they had started the company, they had only focused on their favorite part—the design. Boxes of unopened mail lined their walls. Their finances were a mess. Even their beautiful artwork that they wanted to display with pride was piled in random places.

The first day we began our work together, I sat down with Emmanuel and his top two designers. As they began to tell me the things they needed help with, I noticed something interesting. I'll tell you what they said first, and let's see if you can guess what I noticed.

"Oh Nora, we're so bad. The office is a mess. We have no systems, no structures. We're terrible business people. We're just terrible." Emmanuel was distraught.

"I don't see it that way, but go on," I said.

"We have no clue what's happening with our finances—the bank balance will be $500,000 one week and then $35,000 the next. We think we're batting it out of the park, and then we can barely make payroll."

"That sounds tough," I said.

"It's just so embarrassing."

"I hear you," I said. "Can I ask you a question?"

"Uh, sure," Emmanuel was anxious, but he was willing to be brave.

In as gentle a voice as I could, I asked, "Can you tell me what's happening with the mail?"

Emmanuel's colleague Javier piped up, "Oh Nora, we are SO BAD. We never open the mail. Oh God, we're so bad."

Can you guess what I heard? I heard that they were beating the heck out of themselves for things they either had no training for or things that totally overwhelmed them.

"The first thing I'm going to tell you," I said soothingly, "is that you are **not bad**. I've seen hundreds of people struggling with exactly these same issues. These issues don't mean you're bad. They mean you've never been trained to feel good while you're taking care of these things in ways that keep you and your business healthy."

Over the next few weeks, I taught them the basics of financial tracking, and we worked together to organize their office physically in a way they would like. But the most important things I taught them were not the new skills. They could have learned those from a YouTube video. The most important things I taught them had to do with making a playground for achieving their mini-units of activity.

We started that day, actually.

"Listen," I said, "I want to blow your mind about this mail thing. You say you can't make yourself open it. Could you open a piece of mail with me sitting right here?"

Ishwara (the other designer at the meeting) grabbed a piece of mail and ripped open the envelope. Then Javier, Ishwara and Emmanuel figured out what to do with it in a matter of seconds and it was gone.

"Wow, you did it!"

"Yes, but only because you're here, Nora."

"That's OK for this moment, but I'm going to teach you something that will expand your independence right now."

They looked skeptical.

"Could we set a timer for 10 minutes and all open mail together just for those 10 minutes?"

"But what about all the boxes?" asked Ishwara.

"Boxes get cleared out one minute at a time. I'm just asking for 10. Oh, and could we put on some rock music while we're doing our 10 minutes?"

Emmanuel gasped, "We're allowed to do that?"

"Emmanuel," I said, "you're allowed to do anything you want as long as it's legal and it helps you get your work done."

I set the timer on my phone for 10 minutes and we put on some lively rock music. It was fun to sway to the music with Emmanuel, Javier and Ishwara as they opened and sorted mail.

When the 10-minute timer went off, I called out, "Two-minute dance break!" and they all looked at me like I had three heads.

"What? I thought you guys liked to dance."

"We love to dance, but," Emmanuel paused, "we're allowed to do that?"

"Guys," I said, "work is supposed to be fun. Are we taking this two-minute dance break or what?"

All four of us danced around the office until the two-minute timer went off.

"What do you say? Another 10 minutes of mail and two minutes of dancing?"

And they all enthusiastically agreed.

We worked on numerous other issues during the time I worked with them. But I'm delighted to report that all their mail was sorted and put away within a matter of weeks.

A Nora Story: Discovering Fun

After getting the support I needed to release blame and look for my part, my friends started encouraging me to take action to find a new job.

I was terrified of getting fired again. And even with all my new awareness, I wasn't sure how that would translate into results.

I was lucky enough to qualify for unemployment after getting fired from that third job in 2006. And I had become so careful with money (since I had so little) that I was actually able to save money. It sounds a little weird, I know. But lentils, oatmeal, and living in cheap sublets with lots of roommates in the most obscure locations helped a lot.

So I had a little breathing room. I went to a lot of support group meetings and asked for a lot of help.

One friend suggested that I make a list of all the things I liked to do. So I tried that. I had a lot of time on my hands so the list was about five pages long. It included things like tap-dancing, writing poetry, talking to people, answering phones, researching global politics, writing theories of existence, singing, comedy improv, and reading about the stock market. Let's just say it was a list with a lot of variety.

After reading the list out loud to a few friends, I realized something. Every single one of these things falls into two categories: I love people. And I love writing, words, and ideas.

Then I called a bunch of friends and asked, "People and writing, writing and people, how do you make money at that?"

There were a lot of folks who could tell me how to be low-paid editors and writers. There were a few who could tell me how to be slightly better paid receptionists. This question nagged at me.

Then, I thought, I know! I'll write a book about abundance! There I was, living so frugally that I could save money on unemployment, and I thought I was going to become some abundance and money guru. Wasn't I cute?

When I sat down with two friends, John and Delilah, to talk about my plans, I started to explain the situation. "It's been about three months since I was fired, and I have about three months left before unemployment runs out."

They nodded their heads. "Go on," said my friend John.

"My plan is to publish this abundance book and make a lot of money. But my fear is that I might not get my big juicy book advance before unemployment runs out, and I don't have a lot of savings."

Now they both looked puzzled. John spoke first, "Nora, has your book been accepted by a publisher?"

"No."

"Have you submitted a book proposal anywhere?"

"I'm working on my book proposal now. I know when I finish it, the right person will arrive."

"Do you know anyone in the publishing industry?"

"No. But I have faith!"

Delilah looked me up and down and took a deep breath.

"Nora," she said, "I'm going to tell you something you don't want to hear."

I was a little scared now but I tried to keep smiling anyway.

"Nora, you're arrogant. You don't want to work."

I was surprised by how good it felt to hear her say that. I think because it was the truth.

"You're absolutely right, Delilah. I don't want to work, I'm terrified of working."

"But you need to work, Nora, you need to be able to take care of yourself no matter what your dreams are."

I got quiet. "I know you're right. I'm just so scared of failing again."

Then John piped up, "You know, Nora, the best wisdom I've heard is NOT 'Do what you love and the money will come.' It's **'Do whatever you have to do to TAKE CARE OF YOURSELF. Learn to show up**

with integrity and maturity and love and compassion. And, slowly but surely, you'll be guided to earn a healthy income doing what you love.'"

(NOTE: John was right about this...within a year I was doing work I enjoyed for a good salary. Within two years, I was earning six figures at this work. Within five years, I was earning six figures as a business owner helping people and businesses earn more money—which was my dream when I walked into that meeting with my plan to be an abundance guru. Pretty cool, right?)

Now back to the conversation with John and Delilah...

"OK," I said to them, "what do I need to do?"

"Have you started looking for a J-O-B?" Delilah asked.

"I've been calling people and asking about jobs but...wait, stop...NO, the truth is I've been avoiding looking for work as much as I can."

"Good girl, the truth will set you free!" said Delilah.

"Why do you think you've been avoiding looking for a new job, Nora?" asked John.

And all of a sudden, I knew something I hadn't known until that very moment.

"Because in my heart of hearts, I'm afraid that if I find a job I love, I'll be paid really badly and be miserable and poor. And if I find a job that pays well, I'll be doing boring work I hate. I guess I don't believe I can love a job and be paid well. Wow, it feels so good to say that out loud."

John smiled. "Do you know that I love my job AND I get paid well?"

"No," I said, "I didn't know that."

Then Delilah said, "Nora, lots of people earn good money and love their jobs."

"Really? Who?" This "work-is-boring" belief felt deeply true for me back then.

"I don't think our job is to prove to you that it's possible," she said. "I think it's our job to help you find what you can do to make it possible for you."

"Go home and write a list," she said, "of all the qualities you want in a job."

I was skeptical. "A list?"

"Yes, a list. And, ask for a lot. Because you'll be angry that you didn't ask for more when the universe delivers things you thought were impossible. Write the amount of money you want to make. Write the location you want to be in. Write the qualities of the people you want to work with. Write everything you can think of."

"Definitely write the list," said John, "and then let's set a date when you'll actually start looking for work. Go ahead and take the weekend to finish your book proposal since it's important to you."

I wanted to tell him that my book proposal sounded like a crazy fantasy at that point but I kept my mouth shut.

"Then, how about you start your job hunt on Monday the 15th?"

Monday January 15, 2007. A day that would change my life forever.

But first...

The Magic Begins

It was the famous science fiction writer Arthur C. Clarke who said, "Any sufficiently advanced technology is indistinguishable from magic."

On January 15, 2007, I didn't understand how powerful the nervous system was both to limit and to expand our perceptions—and therefore, our reality.

In fact, I wouldn't understand it as science for a very long time.

Even now...

Now that I have found research from neuroscience studies across the world that completely support my theories...

Now that I have found data from some of the most impressive institutions in the world, including Harvard and Stanford and Columbia...

Now that I've seen my theories work for thousands of people...

Even now, I'm certain that the amount of knowledge we have about the human brain and nervous system is a tiny sliver of what we're going to learn over the next 20 to 30 years.

So, be prepared for some magic I can explain and some magic I can't explain to you as much as I would like, OK?

But nevertheless, I hope you're excited for some magic!!

Delilah's List

When the morning of January 15, 2007 arrived, I woke up and got ready for the day. I called a few morning check-in buddies from my tribe. I had breakfast. I wrote in my journal and wrote a few feel-good affirmations.

Then, it was time to keep my commitment and start my job search. I had no idea what to do first. I picked up the list I had made over the weekend at Delilah's behest and said a quiet prayer: "God, please show me what you want me to do first."

Just then, the thought occurred to me to compose a new affirmation based on Delilah's list, using a special affirmation structure I had made up a few years before.

I began to write: Thank you God for...

Thank you God for...

For what? A hippy-dippy friend of mine had told me that you had to write an affirmation five times for it to work. Whatever I came up with, I decided I would write it five times.

Suddenly I had it:

Thank you God for my fascinating, interesting, high-paying, abundant job you send me with grace and ease.

I felt light-headed. My nervous system did not like that I was trying to re-program myself around scary job fears.

But I didn't care, I wrote it again.

Thank you God for my fascinating, interesting high-paying, abundant job you send me with grace and ease.

I felt a little more grounded, a little more excited.

Thank you God for my fascinating, interesting high-paying, abundant job you send me with grace and ease!

I was really buzzing now.

Thank you God for my fascinating, interesting high-paying, abundant—

And suddenly, the phone rang. It was the recruiter who had helped me get the most recent job I'd been fired from a few months earlier.

I didn't think I would ever hear from her again. I was so embarrassed by the way I had disappointed her by getting fired from that job. If I hadn't been feeling so good from writing that affirmation, I might have avoided her call altogether.

Instead, when I answered the phone, she told me about a job in the research department of an executive search firm. It was a job that included the opportunity to advance to full recruiter if I performed well.

"Retained executive search? Is that kind of like what you do?"

"Kind of. But you're dealing with higher-level positions at companies."

I had loved the experience of having a recruiter place me in my previous job. Nothing like that had ever happened to me before. In the intervening months, I had sent this recruiter more than 20 people to add to her database. All she did all day was talk to people and help them get jobs. If this job was anything like hers, I wanted to try it.

"I'm totally interested," I told her.

Four days later, I walked into the Park Avenue office of a tiny eight-person executive search firm. To me, this office was fancy and business-like.

The woman who interviewed me seemed to like me a lot. Let's call her Owner-Boss-Lady. She told me that the recruiters at her firm talked to high-level executives all day, trying to find the smartest and best ones to match them with her company's clients. She told me that some of these clients were famous companies I had heard of. And that she had placed some of the most senior leaders at these big, famous companies.

I found myself really excited and told her so. "It sounds like a really interesting way to help people," I said. She smiled at me and said in this very no-nonsense New York way, "We're not doctors or lawyers, Nora. If we screw up, nobody dies or goes to jail." I burst out laughing. She cracked me up!

"But we do get to talk to interesting people all day, and if you're any good, you can make A LOT of money."

It was like she had read my affirmation before I got there. I could not wait to start this job!

Since it was my first real job in the business world, she said she would start me in the research department so that I could get a feel for the industry. Then, in about 3 to 6 months, if I had learned enough, I would be allowed to call executives and help recruit them for jobs.

Years later, I understand that many, many people are totally freaked out by cold-calling. But being as ignorant as I was of the whole system, I COULD NOT WAIT to call all these smart people and talk to them about their careers. I prayed that I would be found worthy of being promoted out of research and into the heaven of calling interesting strangers.

I accepted the job on the spot. I was so excited, I went against advice Delilah had given me and accepted her salary and bonus offer right away. I knew how much I needed to cover expenses, and what she was offering would be more than enough. I was so ready!

Tool: Write Your "Things I Love to Do" List

In my story, there were two incredibly important lists for me to make.

The first was a no-limits list of everything I liked to do, as though the world was built around me and only me. The second was a list of all the qualities I wanted in a job—all the components that I thought would make work fascinating and fun. It felt frivolous and playful and delicious to write this list.

I've talked about some difficult things so far:

- Looking at ourselves to understand our defenses.
- Looking at ourselves to understand the lies our nervous systems are telling us.
- Looking at ourselves to see where we're blaming others.
- Looking at ourselves to see where we're beating up on ourselves.
- And looking at ourselves to see where our childhood experiences are coloring our perceptions of reality.

BUT...

What about the things that make us happy?

What about the things we love?

What about the things that make us smile and laugh and get up out of our chairs to dance around to the music in our own heads?

Don't those count too?

The answer is YES! Of course, they do!

Is it any fun to be well-paid and productive at a job you find boring and miserable? NO!!

Am I telling you to quit your boring, miserable job right now? NO!!

Instead, I'm asking you to gently put aside your feelings of boredom and misery about things outside you and start looking inside yourself for the things that bring you joy and fun.

So many of us have TO DO lists. But how many of us have "THINGS I LOVE TO DO" lists?

What I'm asking you to do is go in small, tiny steps (just like I did). All I want you to do at this moment is take out a piece of paper or make a note on your phone and start making a list of all the things you love to do.

This list has no limits. It can include work-related items and non-work-related items. It can sound childish, adult-ish, naughty, clean, responsible, irresponsible, or all of the above.

If it feels kind of frivolous and stupid to spend your time doing this, then you're doing it EXACTLY the right way.

Why? Because our nervous system is constantly on the lookout for things that it can tell us we're doing wrong. If your thoughts are telling you that this list is a bad idea and a waste of time, then, Congratulations! You have an opportunity to truly re-program your own judgmental thoughts toward yourself.

After all, **if making this list is frivolous and wasteful, then being paid well to do even a few of the things that show up on this list must be positively sinful!**

Remember that the nervous system is always looking for the rules that will ensure survival. If you were taught to be a good person, a hard-working person, an honest person, then somewhere in the limited logic of your childhood mind, you probably equated fun and delight with the opposite of good, honest, **_hard_** work.

In fact, most people unknowingly peg guilt and shame to fun and delight. Isn't that...well, isn't that NO FUN?

[For more guidance and super cool tools for writing your "Things I Love to Do List," go to www.getaheadandstayahead.com.]

Laura's Story: You Mean It's OK to Relax?

"This is all well and good, Nora," Laura told me after I'd finished telling her the story of my fun lists, affirmations and remarkable experiences of January 2007. "But how does it apply to me?"

Laura was a sales rep for a very large and well-known software company. She was already one of the top sales reps in the company and was easily earning in the high six figures.

She had hired me because she knew she could earn more (her bosses had told her so) but she was hitting a ceiling around her time, her stress, and her sense that work was just no fun anymore.

"Writing certain words and phrases is one of the fastest and most powerful tools for re-programming the reality that your nervous system can perceive around you." I told her.

"Look, I've done affirmations before, and I understand their benefit," she said. "They make you feel good about yourself; they help you soothe yourself from inner child stuff...I've been in therapy, Nora. And this stuff was part of it. And I do feel like I grew..."

"I feel like there's a **but** coming," I said.

"Buuuut...how does any of this feel good hippy-dippy stuff help me earn more money and feel less stressed? I get how it makes me feel good, but how can it do anything beyond that?"

"I'm so glad you asked, Miss Laura. I do not believe that all affirmations make us feel good. I think a lot of them make us feel like phony, silly liars. Years ago, I remember staring into the mirror and saying *I am a money magnet* over and over again. I just felt stupid...it didn't change anything for me.

But I heard enough people talk about how well affirmations worked for them that I kept experimenting until I discovered the structure I use now for myself and my clients. I discovered the structure before I understood the science behind it. But now that I'm a neuroscience nerd, I can explain to you in pure scientific terms why these structures work—what to expect of them and what not to expect of them."

"All right," Laura said, "I'm listening."

"Remember that the world is very big. Bigger than our tiny human brains will ever be able comprehend. The number of potential realities in this vast world is infinite. There are literally millions and billions of perceptions and interpretations out there that somebody somewhere has had or is going to have someday. Did the laws of physics exist before Newton wrote them down? Was travel to the moon possible before anyone started talking about it? There are so many possibilities and realities out there waiting for us to discover them—it blows my mind to think about it.

"But in this big beautiful world of ours, all we see is the tiny sliver that our eyes and brains and nervous systems tell us is there. This tiny sliver is based on our childhood experiences when our nervous system's number one goal was to identify pain and danger so that it could learn to defend us from whatever threats were in our environment. After all, in ancient times, some people had to deal with saber-toothed tigers, others with grizzly bears, others with elephants—and those different threats require different skills for survival.

"So we don't actually see the world as it is. We see the world as WE ARE—or more specifically—we see the world as our nervous system survival programming thinks we need to see it.

"You and I have already talked about the fact that you grew up with a lot of drama and anger around money from your parents when you were a kid. And it's important to talk out those underlying issues in order to give you the support, listening, and healing you deserve.

"But if we want to change your experience of your own reality, then we have to give your nervous system access to new versions of reality. Those new versions of reality have to come from that great, big unknowable, infinite world...because they aren't going to come from inside your survival-mode-perceptions based on being a vulnerable child in a dangerous home.

"Yeah," said Laura, "how do we switch from survival mode to growth mode?"

"Well, I believe that the easiest way for our nervous system to process and relate to the infinite realities out there is to call all those realities 'God.' Some people have issues with the word 'God' so for those people, it might be a notion of infinite love or a big loving universe.

"The first step is to switch from a negative unknown to a positive unknown. For some people who are cool with the 'God' word, that means switching from a negative, limiting God who is constantly judging and punishing you to a loving, adoring, nurturing God who only wants to give you the biggest and the best if you're ready to receive it."

"What do you mean if I'm ready to receive it?" Laura was suddenly a little miffed. "Obviously I want to receive it."

"Not as much as you'd think," I told her. "Whenever we come up against a limit that seems hard to overcome, that's usually because receiving what's on the other side of that limit scares us somehow.

"Think about the people who receive a lot of money and success before they're mature enough to handle it responsibly...child stars, young professional athletes, music prodigies. So many of them get hurt or lose their way because they don't have the healthy inner resources to stay grounded and take good care of the external resources that have been entrusted to them. Believe me, you are lucky if your nervous system is smart enough to push those things away before you're ready to grow into the healthy, responsible adult who can take care of them with maturity. The last thing I would wish for you would be to die of a drug overdose like River Phoenix or John Belushi."

"Now you're scaring me a little, Nora."

"It can be scary. But the good news is that the work we do using the other tools I'll give you will help you continue to grow into that mature, healthy responsible steward of all the financial, emotional and spiritual wealth you seek. So the growth will have many dimensions but just so you know, the words and phrases I give you will be one tool that will be a very powerful ingredient in your overall growth."

She looked me up and down. "So, basically, what you're saying is that affirmations by themselves are hit or miss at best. But the Nora-version of affirmations is uniquely effective, especially because they are part of a larger Nora toolset?"

"That, Laura, is exactly what I'm saying."

"OK, I'm buying what you're selling, let's keep going."

"Cool. Let's get back to the idea of the infinite realities world that certain humans like to call God, and other humans like to call universe or love or infinity or whatever. I don't want you to worry too much about what's really out there. The only thing I know for sure about the world outside me is that my tiny little nervous system can't perceive very much about it at all.

"Instead, I want you to think of your interactions with this God/universe/love force as your nervous system's easiest way to open up to realities it has never experienced before. Because the reality you're willing to accept as real is the reality we're messing with. And that reality begins and ends in your nervous system."

"OK, so what's wrong with my nervous system?" Laura was so feisty. I loved it.

"Nothing's wrong with your nervous system...it's done a terrific job keeping you alive until now. But you don't just want to stay alive...you want to make more sales and feel less stressed, right?"

"Oh God, yes."

"So our job is to get your nervous system interacting with a reality it's never experienced before. A reality where it's easy and fun to be very successful. Are you willing to spend a little time each day writing some words and phrases I give you that will help you gain access to that new reality?"

"OK, yes, let's do this."

And then I walked Laura through the tool below.

Tool: Write Affirmations

The traditional view of affirmations is that they help turn negative thoughts and feelings into positive thoughts and feelings. But the particular contours of our negative thoughts and feelings come from the unique negative patterns we develop as defenses against difficult childhood experiences that color our perceptions. Some people call those experiences wounds.

If I'm spreading affirmations over my negative thoughts and feelings, without dealing with the underlying wounds, then I'm using affirmations to avoid, not heal.

[For more tools to help identify your underlying wounds and recognize the negative beliefs they generated, go to www.getaheadandstayahead.com.]

Healing Is a MUST

For affirmations to work, we have to be willing to heal the underlying pain. That means building a tribe that provides loving, accepting support. It means learning to give and receive gentleness and listening.

It also means looking for the ways that we hurt other people in adulthood by acting out childhood pain (often unknowingly).

I had learned as a child that I was responsible for everyone and everything. Yet, as an adult, all my problems seemed to come from everyone else. My friends and mentors in my support groups showed me that I had it backwards. In childhood, I was not responsible. The pain that I felt from childhood experiences was not my fault. Children deserve love and safety and getting their needs met. When my mom called me fat, ugly, disgusting and worthless, it was not my fault.

Taking Responsibility

Once I left my childhood home, as poorly prepared as I was for a healthy adult life, now I was responsible for my actions and words towards others, towards myself, even towards my mom. No matter what she had done in the past, I had to take responsibility for how I behaved around her and everyone else.

"Self-esteem comes from esteemable acts," a friend had once told me. And he was right. My esteemable acts had to include loving acts towards myself and others.

As much as I had marched into adulthood with the best of intentions, I didn't know how to treat myself or anyone else with honor, integrity and gentleness.

The journey has been a long one and I don't think I'll ever be "done."

Way back in January 2007, all that mattered was that I had signed up for the process. The results were both fast and slow. Because I was practicing honest, humble "esteemable acts," my affirmations DID help me change the childhood survival mechanisms that had held me back as an adult.

The Three-Part Affirmation Structure

Part One:

I always start with the words: "Thank you God for..."

I chose those words because I didn't want to lie. Shouting "I am a money magnet" into the mirror felt like lying. When I started all this, I was broke and terrified, for goodness' sake.

But saying, "Thank you God for…" is a way to practice being grateful and receptive. It allows me to show my nervous system that I am willing to take ownership of recognizing, receiving and taking good care of the gifts that are being sent to me before they arrive.

And it helps me practice the attitude of honor toward people and things that I haven't received before, so that when those things do arrive, being gracious and receptive feels familiar and easy.

Part Two:

Here I would write the opposite of whatever wasn't working for me in my nervous system's current reality. If I was feeling doomed to poverty and misery, then the opposite was "unlimited abundance." If it seemed that work had to be boring or low-paying, then the opposite was "my fascinating, interesting, high-paying, abundant job."

"A loving, nurturing God only has three answers to any request," a spiritual mentor had once told me… "One: 'Yes.' Two: 'Yes, but not now.' And three: 'No, because I have something better.'"

With that in mind, whenever I wrote the Part Two "opposite," I tried to leave it general enough so that the infinite reality beyond my nervous system perceptions could deliver a "No, because I have something better" answer. Because why would I want to allow my narrow imagination to limit what I can receive?

Part Three:

I always ended my affirmations with the words: "you send me with grace and ease." I grew up thinking everything worthwhile in life took hard work, effort, and pain. Everything my mother ever gave me—food, money, attention—she made a big deal of how hard it was to give these things to me. And being perfect and controlled enough to earn love or approval from her took enormous work. The "you send me with grace and ease" part implied that God made it easy for me to receive without a lot of effort.

Every piece of the affirmation was meant to imply that I was dealing with a loving, nurturing Higher Power, who always delivered gifts with as much grace, joy, love, and ease as I was willing to receive. My first, more mortal Higher Power—my mom—had never been able to give to me in this way.

Back to Laura...

"Whether or not you believe in God, how you related to your parents and your world in childhood will shape the limits you perceive on your reality in adulthood. If you would like to make yourself more available to a reality where things are easier, more fun, and less stressful, then the words and phrases you choose must presume a loving, nurturing source of a world just for you that stretches far beyond your current comprehension."

Laura began to tease me, "I don't know how you just used science to convince me that it's easier to use the word God than anything else in these affirmations, but you did it, Nora. So let's get to work."

(Just because Laura was OK with God doesn't mean you have to be. "Thank you universe" works just as well!)

So Laura and I got to work creating her first batch of Nora-style affirmations as specific re-programming tools for her nervous system.

They were:

Thank you God for the unlimited abundance you send me with grace and ease.

Thank you God for guiding me to earn abundantly while serving my clients with integrity, joy, grace and ease.

Thank you God for guiding me to serve my gracious, loving clients easily, effortlessly and profitably.

Thank you God for guiding me to create enormous value for my clients and for myself easily and effortlessly.

Laura wrote each one 10 times per day each day for about five months. And what do you think happened? Because we ALSO did the work on the old childhood pain stuck in her nervous system AND gave her new tools for interacting with clients and colleagues, the affirmations were an incredibly potent tool. Her clients got bigger. Her paychecks got bigger. Her team got bigger. Her bosses got happier. And she was pretty darn delighted by the whole experience.

Your Turn

Would you like to try using the three-part affirmation structure to expand what your nervous system can recognize, receive and take good care of?

Would you like to add or subtract a part based on your own child/parent patterning?

Remember, the ways your parents behaved around money, food, love, clothes, schoolwork, grades, and all kinds of other resources will color most of how you experience money and work now. Look inside yourself for those old memories, and look for the way the world looks because of those old memories. Now, let's begin to access a reality beyond your current perception.

Here are a few samples:

If you believe work has to be hard and difficult...

Thank you Universe for guiding me to be of service at work with ease, grace and fun.

If you believe people make work hard and difficult...

Thank you Infinite Love for surrounding me with love, peace, connection and fun in every moment of the day at my job easily and effortlessly.

If you believe it's hard to get clients...

Thank you God for the easy, fun, profitable clients you send me with grace and ease.

If you believe your boss is no fun...

Thank you Spirit for guiding me to relax and enjoy the miracles of human connection and communication with my boss easily and effortlessly.

Please use the words and names and phrases that you find inspiring. At various times, I've written anywhere from 1 to 15 different affirmations in at least 10 repetitions each per day.

Remember, the whole point of this exercise is to give you concrete actions for training your brain to be available for realities it has not experienced before, especially around money and work.

You can use this Affirmation Tool around many of the lies that we're blasting through in this book. But please remember that these affirmations are only the beginning of re-programming your work perceptions. Affirmations are designed to help you shift your nervous system's awareness and perceptions of the world around you. However, in order to create real change, your nervous system requires new actions and experiences as well.

Throughout the book, I'll continue to give you action-oriented tools to combine with affirmations so that you take new action consistent with the healthier perceptions you've now started to choose through affirmations.

Combining awareness of your old underlying nervous system responses with affirmations designed to create healthier internal programming and then adding new action skills at work will turbocharge your growth in the most delightful and enjoyable ways.

The Science of Physical Writing

In terms of how you repeat or write affirmations, I've heard of many different approaches: speaking into a mirror, typing, texting, and plenty of others. In my experience, the most effective method by far is physically writing the affirmations with a pen or pencil on a pad or piece of paper.

I observed the overwhelming effectiveness of physically writing affirmations for myself and my clients for many years before I understood the science behind why it works. Physical writing triggers many components within the nervous system, but I'll boil it down into two bite-size pieces for you.

1) Scientists at the University of Umea, Sweden have shown that there are neurons (powerful brain cells) in our fingertips that are performing calculations as complex as the neurons in the most advanced parts of our brains. So touching and gripping that pen or pencil with your fingers as you write these new thoughts is triggering high-functioning neurons to fire in your fingers as well as your brain. Getting neurons to fire in multiple places in the body is a huge advantage for re-programming your nervous system's capacity to perceive new levels of reality.

2) Scientists in some of the most advanced neuroscience labs in the world are currently conducting research into the interaction and communication between the brain and nerves throughout the body. One of the most exciting experiments has to do with the brain's relationship to nerves in the muscles of the arms and hands. The findings show that the brain does not issue unquestioned commands to nerves in the arms and hands. Rather, the brain sends signals to the hands and arms about how to move AND the hands and arms send signals to the brain about how they "want to move."

In the words of one of my scientist buddies, "It's not the old model of brain-in-command and nerves following orders. And it's not a free-for-all. It's more like a negotiation—distributed control." This means that if your hand is writing these positive words, your brain will be listening in ways scientists in the lab are only now beginning to understand. Pretty cool, right?

[For more on how to get the most out of your written affirmations, go to www.getaheadandstayahead.com for extra guidance and tools.]

Lie #4: If I'm Procrastinating, Something Is Wrong

Oh, procrastination, that tempting mistress! What, oh, what is to be done about procrastination?

A lot, actually.

First of all, procrastination isn't bad or wrong. It's common, healthy and normal for a human nervous system in our modern society to procrastinate—a lot.

The trouble is procrastination can really get in the way of achieving our goals. And we tend to have a sneaking feeling of guilt and shame as we're procrastinating—even when we're doing something fun—because so many of us think that work can't be fun, right? Then, when we're finally scared enough to sit down and work, we tend to judge ourselves for procrastinating, which brings us back to telling ourselves we're no good. And if we're feeling no good, then it's really easy to blame that feeling on other people.

So I'm not here to beat up on you for procrastinating. Procrastination is a gateway drug to the hard stuff like self-loathing and resentment. But I think you'll actually love getting sober from this gateway drug. It's a life-changing experience to re-program your nervous system around procrastination. Believe me.

A Nora Story: Addicted to Procrastination?

After I accepted my cool new recruiting firm research job, I started to get very nervous. What if I screwed it all up...again? I had looked at my role in my past failures and found all kinds of childhood issues. But what about my actual moment-to-moment actions? What if there were things I didn't even know I was doing that were keeping me from being successful?

Thank goodness I had a tribe of people to support and love and validate me through my fear **so that I could get to the other side of my fear and make new discoveries.** With the strength of my loving tribe encouraging me and helping me stay away from beating up on myself, I began to look at my actual day-to-day actions at these three jobs.

At all three, I procrastinated a lot. Like *a lot*. But it turned out I only used three things to do all that procrastination:

1) Personal email
2) Personal internet surfing
3) Personal phone calls/texting

That was it. Just three. But when I began to write down how often I had done those three things instead of my work, I was actually amazed to discover that I was spending about 3 to 6 hours per day on these three simple things. No wonder I wasn't getting any work done!

Did I go to work thinking that I would spend 3 to 6 hours per day avoiding work? Of course not! I went to work with a desire to create value and serve others. But I'll be darned if I could get my actions to match my intentions.

My internal monologue would go something like this:

I'm here at my desk...let's get started with that project. Oh yes, here it is, uh-huh, uh-huh, ooh, let me do that right now. Yay I did it! That was easy. OK, next would be figure out that Excel formula. Ugh, I'm not sure how that goes and Sarah isn't at her desk yet to explain it to me.

Let me just check my email for a second...Oh look, my friend Katya wrote me! Ooh, what did she say...ooh, this is long...(read, read)...ooh this requires a really thoughtful response (type, type).

<Sarah walks in>

"Hi Sarah! How was your weekend?"

Let me get back to typing this email to Katya. Oh good, I'm finished. Let me read it for typos. Oh, I've said some powerful stuff. She'll like it. OK,

Send. Oh look, Samantha wrote back to my big cry fest email about my mom (read, read), oh look, Katya, wrote me back! So soon! (read, read).

And so on. And so on.

Three hours later, while Sarah was at lunch, I would remember that I needed her help with the Excel formulas and then I would check the online news stories and the cycle would begin again. Then a friend would call...

I never intentionally ignored my work. I just kept taking it one email at a time, one interesting article at a time, one important phone call at a time. Before I knew it, the day was over.

And that was how I had lost three jobs in six months.

Bet You Can't Do Just One!

My nervous system was great at telling me that I was just doing one really important distracting action. And then one more, and then one more, and then one more. But this was its way of lying to me. I wasn't doing one, I was doing many. It was the way I would lie to myself about slices of pizza or brownies or slices of bread as a compulsive overeater.

The only thing that had worked for me to break my overeating patterns was to admit that I had an addiction to food and that I needed help from other food addicts to set limits on my food each day before I ever took a bite.

Could it be that I was addicted to distraction the way I was addicted to food? This blew my mind.

Tool: Noticing Distraction

What's your favorite thing to do at work that's not work?

Is it chit-chatting at the water cooler?

Watching fun online videos?

Surfing Facebook?

Posting something hilarious on Twitter?

Taking a snack break?

It's not bad to take time for yourself at work. We all need to take the edge off, right?

Another question is: What's your favorite thing to do BEFORE you start a big project?

Is it tidy up your desk? Call a friend? Deal with a personal matter?

We all need little breaks to lower blood pressure and keep ourselves sane when we're dealing with the little and big stresses that come up around work. And they always come up, don't they?

So, I'm not asking you to stop taking your breaks or stop cleaning before you start a big project.

And I'm not asking you to judge yourself at all for any time you spend interrupting or procrastinating at work.

What I am asking you to do is NOTICE when you're doing it.

I love to give this exercise to clients, and now I'm going to give it to you. Keep a Post-it note on your desk and write down how many times throughout the day you interrupt yourself for non-work stuff. Just write it down. There's nothing wrong or bad writing it down.

I just want you to NOTICE.

[For more tools to help you notice your personal distractions, go to www.getaheadandstayahead.com.]

More Nora Story: Cold Turkey

As the start date of my new recruiting researcher job neared, my newfound awareness of my addiction to personal email, internet and phone calls began to grow in my mind. What if I lost control at this job the way I had lost control in all the others? How could I keep myself from being the unreliable, unproductive employee I now knew myself to be?

The night before my first day, I finally accepted what I knew I had to do. In the morning, on my way to the job, I called a friend and said, "Just for today, just for this one solitary day, I'm committing to you that I will do NO personal email, NO personal internet, and NO personal phone calls between the hours of 9 a.m. and 5:30 p.m."

"That sounds pretty stark, Nora. Are you sure you want to commit to that?"

My mind was made up. "Yes, I am. I've seen other people check their personal email for five minutes and get right back to work. I can't do **just five minutes of personal email** just like, as a compulsive overeater, I can't have **just a few bites of sugar**."

(As a compulsive overeater, once I have a bite of sugar, I can't stop eating it for a scary amount of time—that's why I don't eat it. If I never start eating it, I'll never have to deal with stopping—kind of the way alcoholics can't have just one drink.)

"If I start on personal email or internet at work, I don't know if or when I'll be able to stop. And I just can't afford to get fired again. I gotta go cold turkey."

The Pain That Changed My Life

I arrived at the office and was welcomed nicely. When introductions were over, they gave me a stack of simple background reading and data entry tasks to get me started. With utter determination, I marched the pile over to my new desk and began the first task. I finished it within a few minutes and went to reach for the second task when I heard a little voice in my head say, "Check your email! See who loves you! Take the edge off!"

I paused in my chair, but then I gently reminded myself that I had committed to no personal email, internet or phone calls, just for this one day. When I turned back to the pile of work, I felt a shooting pain in my gut. It was as though someone had punched me in the stomach. "Holy mackerel," I thought, "what was hiding underneath this distraction?"

The pain was intense but I managed to pick the second assignment up off the pile with weak, clammy hands. As I began reading, the pain lessened ever so slightly. As I got a little more absorbed in the subject matter, the pain continued to decrease until it was non-existent.

When I finished the second task, the pain came flooding back. But this time it was just a tiny bit less intense than the first time. "Breathe," I told myself, "honor your commitment—it's just for this day, just for this one day."

As I became absorbed in task #3, the pain once again began to subside and I was happily focused on my work. But as I neared completion of the task, I began to feel anxious about the pain that I knew would come between task #3 and task #4.

I had felt horrible pain like this only once before—when I began to abstain from life-threatening compulsive eating with the help of a lot of other food addicts who had done the same. In my very early days of learning to finish a normal-size meal and then stop eating until the next normal-size meal, the pain I felt when a meal came to an end was horrendous. But being willing to feel that pain instead of escape into food had saved my life. Now, I suspected, this echo of that earlier horrendous pain was going to be equally valuable if I could resist running from it with my distracting actions.

When I finished task #3, I rushed to the pile for the fourth task. The pain was there again, but this time, I started working furiously to see how quickly I could become absorbed in the work and forget the pain again.

I did this little dance with my pain all day. When I ran out of tasks in my pile, I immediately requested more stuff to do so that I didn't have to spend too much time in the soul-searing fire of "in-between."

As I walked out of the office at the end of the day, I felt like I had battled a terrifying demon and come out alive. I called a bunch of friends in quick succession to share the experience and discoveries of the day. The night felt flooded with gratitude and awe.

On Day 2, I made the same commitment and engaged in the same pain dance all day. It was slightly easier than Day 1, as long as I could find work to do as quickly as possible once a task was finished. Again, I felt like a gladiator as I left the office. The exhilaration was immense. I was actually looking forward to making my commitment again on Day 3. And that's just what I did the next morning.

On Day 3, about halfway through the morning, I went back to my boss to ask for more work for the umpteenth time in three days.

"Hmmm. Actually, that was all the work we were going to give you in the first three months. Wanna start making calls?"

I was breathless. Making calls meant talking to smart, interesting executives. Making calls meant getting a promotion. Making calls meant being a recruiter. I began call training that day.

As I strolled out of the office that night and started calling friends to share the day's adventure, I couldn't believe how things had turned around for me in such a short time. That little question: "Wanna start making calls?" was the first time I'd ever been promoted at a job. Could it be that my willingness to feel all that pain had not only made me more productive than my old self, but made me more productive than most people?

I continued to make that commitment of no personal email, phone or internet, one morning at a time, for the next nine months. By consciously abstaining from the triggers that fed my procrastination, just one day at a time, my nervous system developed new skills that forever changed the way that I was able to do work for the rest of my life.

The Saber-Toothed Tiger at Work

Procrastination is a funny thing. It's something we say we do a lot. But while we're doing it, how often do we know it's happening?

My wild experiments in going cold turkey off the three things that were my favorite non-work activities taught me a lot about the way my brain lied to me.

The first thing I learned was that I had a lot more fear, pain and discomfort around doing simple things than I realized. This was really hard to admit. It made me feel like a baby who couldn't be independent or reliable. Honestly, it made me feel worthless to think about how much pain and fear I had around things that were "no big deal."

Now, as I've carried these tools to others, I've discovered that every human being has pain and fear about work stuff in ways that "don't make sense." Work today is like hunting woolly mammoth in caveman times. It's how we put food on the table. Our bodies are still acting like we have to be ready to fight for our lives during the workday the way we would if we were hunting in the wilderness.

I know that sounds extreme. I want you to call to mind the moments when you feel nervous, stressed, annoyed. Those feelings are created by the same chemicals in your body that told your ancestors to run from saber-toothed tigers and forest fires.

I believe procrastination is our modern way of running away from the task that our nervous system tells us might actually be a saber-toothed tiger.

OK, here's the good news: Your nervous system actually CAN TELL THE DIFFERENCE between a saber-toothed tiger and a Word document.

But it's so important to understand that your nervous system **CAN NOT** TELL THE DIFFERENCE between FEAR of a saber-toothed tiger and FEAR of a Word document.

One of the things I learned about myself as I went cold turkey off personal email, internet and phone calls was that I was always a little more nervous about a task BEFORE I was doing it than WHILE I was doing it. Why? Because before I was doing it, it might be a saber-toothed tiger hiding in a data entry computer program. While I was doing it, I was pretty sure that nope, there was no saber-toothed tiger. Just a data entry computer program.

You've probably heard that procrastination is related to anxiety and fear. But fear of what?

Some people think it's fear of DOING. But I don't think that's it. I think it's fear of STARTING.

Starting the new task is like when our ancestors traveled to a new part of the forest looking for animals to hunt or berries to pick. Would there be bears or bobcats waiting for us in this unknown part of the wilderness? Thousands of years later, our system is still protecting us from the saber-toothed tigers that **could be** hiding under that desk and behind the computer screen.

Once we've spent a little time experiencing the new task, we see that we are safe. We see that DOING the actual work can go pretty quickly and easily. And get this: we even get to have fun!

Tool: Find Your Saber-Toothed Tiger at Work

What tasks do you most resist STARTING?

Are they new tasks you're not as familiar with?

Are they tedious tasks that take a lot of steps?

Are they tasks that require collecting information and actions from a bunch of different people you can't always rely on?

Start noticing when you're resisting STARTING something.

Where are the saber-toothed tigers hiding when you imagine doing that task?

Remember, our nervous systems are on the lookout for saber-toothed tigers anytime there's an unknown, unpredictable element that we haven't experienced before. Whenever we're not sure what we'll have to do to survive a new experience, our sensitivity to threats (even imagined threats) is extremely high.

Lawrence's Story: I'm Gonna Get to It

Lawrence was a brilliant and hard-working gastroenterologist who was just starting up his private practice with several partners in a major Midwestern City.

He had the patience to engage in some of the most tedious tasks we put doctors through in this country, God bless him. From memorizing vast swaths of anatomy and physiology to unending paperwork at his hospital, the guy was relentless.

So I was surprised when, as he and his partners began to build their private practice, Lawrence seemed to have a strong resistance to documenting his appointments, and was falling further behind every day.

He and his partners had so many other actions to coordinate in launching their practice that I didn't notice this hidden pocket of procrastination for a while. After all, they had all hired me to help them on issues related more to strategy and communication.

But I like to keep tabs on how the whole project is going, especially when a new venture is launching.

At first, when I asked him about it, all he said, was "I'm gonna get to it. I'm gonna get to it." But then he really wouldn't, even after many other tasks had long been completed.

Finally one day, I asked him, "Lawrence, what is the experience like for you when you do your online record-keeping?"

"Oh, I'm gonna get to it, I really am."

"I know you will. But I'm not as concerned about that right now. What I'm curious about is what actually happens when you sit down to start typing information. Can you explain it to me?"

Out of nowhere, the unruffled composure he had brought to so many of our conversations disappeared.

"Oh, it's the worst!! Every time I want to do the simplest action, I have to take an online video tutorial before I'm allowed to do it. Or sometimes, I need the program to do a very simple function...but then I spend 45 minutes discovering that, nope!! Nope!! That function doesn't exist."

I started to giggle. His shift was so radical it caught me off guard.

"What?!?!?! It's SOOOOO frustrating!!!"

"I totally get that, Lawrence, I really do. It sounds like the unknown, unpredictable learning curve of this online records system is showing up to your nervous system like a big fat saber-toothed tiger. Do you know what we do to fend off saber-toothed tigers?"

"No, what?"

"We bring more hunters into the clearing with us. Can you ask a friend to be your study buddy and just keep you company quietly on speakerphone while you both get some annoying work done together?"

"Actually, that sounds like a great idea," said Lawrence.

And that's exactly what Lawrence did. Within a few weeks, he had totally figured out his online record system. Entering data still felt tedious at times. But those unknown unpredictables had all been conquered in a very short time.

Your Turn

How are you like Lawrence?

What unpredictables are hiding in your to-do list that your nervous system thinks COULD be a saber-toothed tiger?

Can you go gather some fellow hunters to keep you company as you go find those imaginary saber-toothed tigers kick their butts?

I bet you can.

The 3-Minute Bridge

Now let's talk about how long it takes to get through the saber-toothed tiger fear of starting the new task (a.k.a. going to a new part of the forest)?

In other words, how long does it take to transition from STARTING to DOING?

About 3 minutes.

So many of my clients are baffled when I tell them the secret...it really is only 3 minutes. Let's call it the 3-minute bridge.

Imagine that you're living in ancient times and you're about to venture into a part of the forest you've never visited before. Will there be tigers there? Bears? Wolves? During the first few seconds that you venture into this unknown territory, you have to be on high alert. Then slowly, as you look around, you discover that you're in a safe part of the forest. No animals to eat you here. Just yummy berries to pick and bring back to the cave to share with your tribe.

My guess is that the time from cautiously entering the new part of the forest to happily gathering berries for your family would last about 3 minutes.

So, the time from the moment you start a new task to the moment you settle into peacefully doing it will last about 3 minutes, just like it did for your ancestors.

It doesn't sound like that much time, does it?

Susan's 3-Minute Bridge

"Wait a minute, Nora," said Susan, "That doesn't make sense. I've had work to do where I felt anxious about it all day."

"If you felt anxious all day, my guess is you were thinking about it all day but you didn't start it till many hours in," I told her.

"Sometimes that's true. But oftentimes, I'll start something a bunch of different times but be miserable each time."

"Oh, Susan, I'm so glad you brought that up! I've found that too. What I've found is that it's not that the 3-minute bridge doesn't work; it's that the clock re-sets to zero, every time you interrupt. No matter when you interrupt."

Susan was a high-powered marketing executive for a food company in the Midwest. She came to me because after several years of pretty quick promotions and raises, her career had stalled for seemingly no reason.

Her days had once felt exciting and filled with promise. Now, they dragged on, filled with frustration and anxiety.

Did she have childhood issues that were coming up at work? Absolutely. But she'd been in plenty of therapy and support groups for years. Now with all her self-awareness and insight, she was looking for the ACTIONS that would turn things around.

"If you're going to achieve that sense of flow and fun at work again," I told her, "you're going to have to let yourself live through the 3 minutes uninterrupted on each task that you do. Once you've passed the 3-minute mark uninterrupted, you will get that flow sensation that you used to love about your job."

"I did used to love that flow sensation—but back then I was only responsible for me. Now I have people who report to me, constant emails, and my boss walking in at any moment, not to mention my kids calling from school."

"Well, your kids calling is part of the 24/7 mom job...but with everything else, unless it's a crisis, you can schedule it for later. Turn off email notifications and set an alarm to check them between flow moments.

"When people call or interrupt, ask them very nicely to schedule a time with you later in the day or week. As long as you do it with gentleness, setting boundaries to protect your time will make the DOING part a heck of a lot more fun."

"What if they get mad at me? Or uncomfortable?"

"People train themselves to respond to you based on how you train them. If you are kind, loving and casual about it by saying something like… 'I'm so glad you came by but I'm jamming on a deadline right now. Can we talk at 4 p.m.?' Ninety-nine times out of 100, they'll be fine with it."

Tool: Cross Your 3-Minute Bridge

Are you pulled in a million directions at work? Does it feel like things just don't get done unless your adrenaline is pumping and you're really stressed out?

Anytime you START a task but get interrupted, when you START again, it can take up to 3 minutes to release the anxiety of STARTING and settling into the safety of DOING. Your interruption doesn't have to be a chronic self-sabotaging habit like mine. It may be a very real work-related email, phone call or question from a colleague.

But watch out for thoughts in the middle of the 3-minute bridge that tell you to go do something else. That something else might be personal or work-related. But I invite you to consider that, on some level, **that thought is there to save you from the discomfort of those 3 minutes**.

After all, your nervous system's job is to use pain and fear and discomfort as indicators that it's time to run away from the forest fire or fight the saber-toothed tiger. If you run or fight in the nervous system's world, then you'll probably be safe from all those tigers and fires and bears and tar pits.

So it's only natural that your nervous system will manufacture thoughts that naturally interrupt those 3 minutes of discomfort for reasons that seem very smart and sound.

Here are two vital pieces of information that might change your life forever (really!)...

1) Imagine that the 3-minute bridge is 3 minutes of STARTING discomfort that you pay as a toll in exchange for the lovely, flowing DOING time when you're both productive and happy.

2) When you consistently purchase your lovely, flowing DOING time by paying the 3-minute bridge toll, your 3-minute bridge **will actually shorten**.

Feeling that 3-minute bridge discomfort without running away is like working out a muscle. The more you work it out, the stronger your muscle becomes. It turns out that the rules that apply to your muscles also apply to your thoughts, feelings, actions and growth. Why? Because they are ALL governed by your nervous system.

Isn't that the coolest?

So, at first, your 3-minute bridge will last three minutes.

But the next time you start an interrupted task or a new task, your bridge might only last 2.5 minutes.

Then the next time might be 2 minutes.

Then 90 seconds.

Then 30 seconds.

These days, my 3-minute bridge is only about 15 seconds long. Isn't that amazing?

Would you like one more way to hack it down even faster?

This one's very powerful, so be careful, OK?

First, remember that any anxiety you feel BEFORE you actually START the task is fear of the discomfort itself (because who likes to be uncomfortable? Yuck!).

So even if you notice yourself feeling anxious about STARTING, you can say to yourself: "I am grateful for discomfort because it's part of growth. I am grateful for discomfort because the faster I embrace it, the faster I get to feel the DOING part that feels good."

You can even say, "I EMBRACE this discomfort as I re-train my nervous system to feel happy and safe at work. I LOVE this discomfort because it means I'm training myself for growth and gifts I can't even predict yet."

Remember how I felt like a gladiator the first day that I let the pain be there without running to personal email, internet and phone calls? That feeling of making it through the day and honoring my commitment to myself made me feel LIKE A MILLION BUCKS!

That feeling alone was a reward I could never have expected from being willing to embrace the searing pain of my 3-minute bridge. Hopefully, your pain won't be as searing as mine was. But if it is, remember I'm kneeling beside you. You're not alone. Pain is the ticket to get on the train.

However, I never predicted that my 3-minute bridge would go from 3 minutes down to 30 seconds by Day 3. (It really did shrink that quickly and yours will, too, if you practice as much as I did.)

AND, I invite you to consider that because I focused so keenly on my own actions and difficult feelings without blaming them on any person, place or thing...

AND, because I did not run from my difficult feelings and actions with interruptions or distractions...

I GOT PROMOTED out of the blue!

I can't promise you a promotion or a raise right away, but I can promise that things will start to shift sooner than you expect.

As for Susan...

She took on creating uninterrupted time to give herself the chance to shift from STARTING to DOING.

Sure enough, she began to feel a change at work. Tasks got easier, work got more fun. She worried less and produced more.

Did she still have underlying emotional stuff she was working on? Of course she did, we all do. But within less than three months, things began to shift in her roles and responsibilities at work. Her colleagues adjusted to her new work style, and she began to like her job more and more.

[For more 3-minute bridge magic, go to www.getaheadandstayahead.com]

Lie #5: My Boss Is Crazy

I can't tell you how often, how incredibly often I work with people who hate their bosses. Or bosses who are annoyed with their employees. Or companies where they need me to fix the relationship between the bosses and the workers. It is so common.

So the first thing I usually say to someone telling me that their boss is nuts is: Yes, yes he is. Or, yes, yes she is. And so are you.

Human beings are not reasonable, rational beings. We're just not. We're all a little nuts—mostly because our nervous systems are still biologically programmed to be looking for saber-toothed tigers, forest fires and tar pits.

But really, the only saber-toothed tigers most of us meet anymore are criticism, judgment, yelling, self-righteousness, martyrdom, egomania, lying, manipulation, grandiosity, obsession, perfectionism, blame, overindulgence, procrastination, licentiousness and passive-aggression.

If any of these words describe your boss's behavior, Congratulations! You work for a human being! And I guarantee you all the human beings at your company do at least one, probably more, of the nasty things I listed above—including you!

I apologize if I'm offending you. I'm not trying to hurt your feelings.

I'm just letting you know that the sooner you see how much you have in common with the people who drive you crazy—and the sooner you give yourself and them permission to be lovable, valuable and worthy while still being as weird, crazy and annoying as they are, the sooner you'll start having a lot more fun at work.

Don't worry, I know that just telling you to be compassionate with yourself and others doesn't actually give you the power to change how much you get annoyed by your boss. I have to give you tools and stories and examples.

Understanding Bosses

It's hard for bosses because their workers don't always realize that the higher up in the organization you are, the more bosses you actually have. A lot of these bosses are called customers. Because customers/bosses have the power to give or take away money, they can look very scary to us if we don't have the proper tools to work well with them.

You see, for bosses, employees are often both annoying and scary. After all, the only thing more nerve-racking than a boss or customer who has the power to take away your pay...is someone YOU PAY who has the power to ruin your relationship with the people who pay you. And yet, you still have to pay them! How unfair is that? Yuck! Blech!

I'm not excusing their behavior. I'm just saying that most difficult behavior in humans comes from fear. And when we understand WHY their fear is so strong, it can help us respond a whole lot more effectively than when we're just seeing them as totally crazy or annoying.

Employees, bosses, and customers are all scared of each other in different ways. And what do people do when they're afraid? They demonstrate fear-based, defensive behaviors. Behaviors most of us would like to avoid:

Criticism, judgment, yelling, self-righteousness, martyrdom, egomania, lying, manipulation, grandiosity, obsession, perfectionism, blame, overindulgence, procrastination, licentiousness and passive-aggression.

A Nora Story: Everybody HATES You

I played the role of terrified employee (and passive-aggressive martyr) more than a few times in my early career. But I think the most important time happened right after the last story from my work turnaround journey—where refraining from personal email, internet, and phone got me that delicious promotion after only three days!

Remember that? Well, I'm afraid it wasn't exactly smooth sailing afterward.

So, there I was, flying high. The fastest researcher promoted to recruiter in the two-year history of this tiny little firm. Maybe I was over-confident. Maybe I was just immature.

But I strutted into work every day for the next four weeks, eager to start my call list, eager to face down my STARTING discomfort and have it be VANQUISHED by the joy of DOING.

I was a rock star recruiter, loving my job.

For about four weeks.

On late Friday afternoon at the end of the fourth week, Owner-Boss-Lady called me into her office.

"Nora," she said, squinting her eyes at me, "everybody HATES you."

A shooting pain in the pit of my stomach. Don't cry, don't cry, I thought to myself.

"You're childish, IMMATURE, and disorganized. My 15-year-old daughter is more organized than you."

Gulp. Don't cry. Don't cry.

"AND, you're SO NEEDY! You're constantly interrupting me and demanding my attention. Don't you know I have a job to do? I run this company! I am not at your beck and call!!"

I could barely breathe. Don't cry. Don't cry.

"You obviously need therapy."

After this talk, I would think so.

"And if you don't shape up by next Friday, YOU'RE OUT!!"

Aaaaaaand, we're back. I felt a familiar thud in the base of my gut as my hopes and dreams of success sank into rejection and despair.

Again? I thought I had conquered this stuff. Again?? After all this work and all these days of no personal email, internet and phone? And living through all that pain? And my first-ever promotion at a job?

Again with the threats of being fired?

Again?

"What are you still doing here?!?! Get out of my office! And you better shape up next week. OR ELSE!"

"I'll do my best," I whispered and forced myself to walk out slowly when all I wanted to do was run.

Am I Crazy?

I walked out of the office in a daze—thoughts running through my head. "How did I get here again? Am I crazy to feel as terrified and hurt as I feel right now?

"I'm the one at the scene of all these crimes. Is it me? Is it her? Is she right about me? Am I even more of a total mess than I thought? Am I doomed?"

Please understand that after the track record I had had, something in me was very scared that this was a sign that things were going to go downhill fast.

But even though I didn't understand the nervous system back then, I had learned enough in my journey to focus first and foremost on feelings and try—**TRY**—to withhold judgment.

My friends were much more judgmental—and I loved them for it.

The minute I got away from the building, I started making calls.

"Are you kidding?" a friend said to me. "She said that? You should sue!"

"Quit your job!" another friend admonished. "Get away from that crazy lady."

I felt comforted to hear that other people didn't think that what this lady said was the gospel truth.

Less than an hour later, I was sitting in a support group meeting, when I shared the "Everybody Hates You" story AGAIN.

The room gasped. Maybe this really was something she shouldn't have said to me. But I was still deeply fearful of blaming my problems on others the way I had at every other job. I knew the path of blame would lead me to more failure and more firing.

A crowd of people came over to wish me well after the meeting ended. Many of them advised me to quit my job or file a complaint. I chose to focus on absorbing their loving support without agreeing or disagreeing with their advice.

I traveled home feeling much more grounded, just from the gentleness of the meeting, the hugs and the words of encouragement.

As I let my thoughts turn back to the "Everybody Hates You" conversation, the thing that struck me the most was the difference between my initial perception of Owner-Boss-Lady and my perception of her at that moment.

How did Owner-Boss-Lady turn out to be such a scary person? I thought she was so funny and interesting and cool when I met her. I knew I was going to love working for her. I had felt so much loyalty towards her so quickly. I had wanted so badly to work for her and learn from her as we conquered the world of executive recruiting together.

But in just four weeks, she had revealed a side that was angry and critical—many would say raging.

As I sat on the subway, trying to make sense of what had just happened, a few thoughts occurred to me...

Raging behavior doesn't appear randomly out of nowhere.

Her raging behavior started long before I got there and would continue long after I left.

But I hadn't picked up on any signals at all in the four weeks we had worked together. I hadn't even known where to look. I had been totally blindsided. As I thought back through my four weeks of working for her, I began to realize that there were clues in other people's reactions to Owner-Boss-Lady that I had noticed and misinterpreted as their bad attitude or weird style.

Still, it scared me a little that there was nothing in Owner-Boss-Lady's behavior that had struck me as strange or alarming until the "Everybody HATES You" conversation.

No matter how many times my friends told me how right I was or how wrong Owner-Boss-Lady was, there was something about my utter blindness to her shortcomings that gave me pause.

That night, I realized some things that would determine the course of my growth for the next few months, years and possibly my whole life.

What did I realize?

1) Every job situation I had encountered had been more difficult than the previous one.

2) If I tried to run from Owner-Boss-Lady by getting another job immediately, or just quitting, I would only end up in a worse situation.

3) If I stayed at the job, I had the opportunity of a lifetime to grow and learn the lessons I absolutely NEEDED to learn in order to succeed in my career.

So I decided to do whatever it took to stay until the moment I knew I had learned everything I was meant to learn from this experience.

As I began to look for my first big lesson, I began asking questions about my behavior:

How come I picked this lady? Or more specifically, how come I thought this lady who raged at ALL her employees (I found out later), was the coolest, funniest, sassiest woman I had met in a long time?

It didn't take me very long to see that Owner-Boss-Lady was a dead ringer for the woman who gave birth to me.

A Dead. Ringer.

There's a lot I can tell you about my mother that you haven't heard yet. First of all, she's hilarious. And very sassy. Spunky too. She loves to challenge people and ideas. She loves to challenge herself and expands her mind constantly. She's a voracious, critical reader of fiction, poetry and news.

She's a poet who went back for her MFA at age 66. She was going to be an English professor in her 20s, but when she couldn't make herself finish her dissertation, she said, "To hell with it, I'll go to law school." (This is a famous quote in our family.)

She did become a lawyer. Her first job after law school was for the ACLU in New Orleans, where I grew up. Then she took on voting rights cases and prison condition lawsuits all over Louisiana for many years. And for 10 years, she was a public defender in New Orleans Juvenile Court, representing teenagers arrested for crimes as well as kids of all ages who had been abused and neglected. A survivor of abuse herself, my mother loved fighting for the oppressed and abused underdogs of society.

My mother was the most fascinating, interesting, charismatic, exciting person I knew when I was a child. Because of her uncontrollable rages and deep inner struggles, she was also the scariest and most dangerous person I knew.

Owner-Boss-Lady had fit right into my favorite parts about my mother, and somehow, she also exhibited the same tendencies to rage and insult people out of nowhere for no good reason.

Today, because I understand the nervous system, I know that when people fly into rages, it's because their nervous system is feeling INTENSE discomfort. This discomfort is so painful, it doesn't feel safe to be expressed as a feeling; it has to be expressed as a threat response.

That's all rages are—threat responses. For my mother, the abuse she suffered at such a young age programmed threat responses into her perceptions so early and so deeply, that when her rages came, there was very little she could do to stop them.

I never found out enough about Owner-Boss-Lady's childhood to theorize about the root of her raging threat responses.

What I did discover over time was that whenever Owner-Boss-Lady expressed emotion, stress, or was upset about something I needed, it was because her nervous system told her there was a threat to her survival. That threat could be a shortage of resources (time, money or both). Or it could be a shortage of emotional energy (seeing that I needed her to approve of me when she just didn't have it to give). When Owner-Boss-Lady felt threatened, she tended to scream or criticize.

When I felt threatened back then, I tended to get very needy and scared. So my needy stress response to Owner-Boss-Lady often created an experience that escalated her sense of scarcity. And suddenly, she was fighting even harder for her life (i.e., yelling or criticizing even more) with her next response. Before you knew it, we were both fighting for our lives with anger, people-pleasing, passive-aggression, double-talk, gossip, you name it.

Kathryn: But I Like My Parents...

"Sorry to interrupt you, Nora," said Kathryn, "but I like my parents. We've had some hiccups here and there, but my mother lives with me now. We really do get along." Kathryn was the administrative assistant to Quentin, a famously rage-filled Head of Sales at a large New York company. I had been hired to coach Quentin to help him get his temper under control. As I began to coach him, I had also begun to work with his team.

"I don't think of my boss as resembling my mother or my father."

I thought for a minute. "You know, Kathryn, you're right. My Owner-Boss-Lady's resemblance to my mother was pretty darn extreme. I think I needed extreme intensity like that to help me learn the tools I offer today.

"But even though your boss doesn't resemble your parents with the same similarity that mine did, I still think it's healthy and important to explore what I call the parent/boss connection."

And so I began to explain my theories...

The Parent/Boss Connection

The role of parent in childhood and the role of boss in adulthood have a lot in common. They are both responsible for doling out resources essential for survival. Because real life is messy, those resources are often doled out in unstructured, unpredictable ways. The stakes are high around this resource distribution process because of the emotional urgency of survival.

Let's take a look at those survival resources from parents and bosses...

Ideally, parents give children:

- Food, water, shelter, clothing for nourishment and physical protection.
- Love, validation and approval for self-esteem.
- Attention, focus, care and healthy boundaries for a sense of self-care, independence and emotional security.
- Clear expectations, guidance and appropriate rewards and consequences for learning to negotiate the world.
- Wisdom and life lessons for how to succeed in the world.

Ideally, bosses give employees:

- Payment that allows them to purchase food, water, shelter, clothing, etc.
- Approval for a job well done.
- A clear mission, expectations and context for motivation and strategic thinking.
- Guidance for negotiating and achieving specific goals.
- Mentorship for personal and professional growth.

In my story, my mother's shortcomings and my Owner-Boss-Lady's shortcomings were remarkably similar. But even if your parents were terrific parents, it's easy to mentally put your boss in a parental role because it's so easy to believe that you depend on your boss for many day-to-day survival resources in the work world.

So, **if your parents were difficult**, having a boss who falls short of your expectations may trigger old feelings of pain and fear from childhood. And **if you feel good about parents**, having a boss who falls short of your expectations may give you feelings of abandonment or rejection precisely *because* you've been trained to expect better treatment.

But let's be honest, all parents AND bosses fall short on at least a few of the above items from time to time because nobody's perfect. BUT IT'S NOT INTENTIONAL! When parents and bosses do fall short, it's usually because they're dealing with their own blind spots, fears and insecurities.

Tool: Untangling Your Parents and Bosses

If you are having difficulty with a boss, congratulations! You are a member of a large and illustrious club. If you are committed to transforming that difficulty so that you have a new set of tools for dealing with all kinds of difficult situations and even stopping potential problems before they arise, then you are in a much smaller—and much happier—club.

First, ask yourself what you are looking for from your boss that you're not getting. Is it guidance? Approval? Safety? Reassurance?

It's very normal for people to **start out** seeking appropriate guidance in tasks and approval for good work. But if they don't get it the way they want it, they often shift from healthy communication to parent-seeking **without realizing it.**

If your boss's behavior is disturbing to you in even the slightest ways, then it's possible that those moments of disturbance are the ones where you are parent-seeking without even realizing it.

How Can You Stop Parent-Seeking?

First, make a list of all the tiny disturbing things your boss does.

It might look like this:

- When my boss rolls his eyes at me, it makes me mad. How dare he treat me like that?

- When my boss shouts for me to come into her office without looking up from her desk, it makes me feel worthless. How can she be so insensitive towards me?

- My boss interrupts me and tries to finish my sentences even when he doesn't know what he's talking about. What a crummy way to support me in sharing my opinion!

Now look at the list and ask yourself how you would feel if you saw a parent doing those things to a child.

Some of them would make you feel pretty angry and sad, right?

Your boss is picking up on those angry, sad feelings—whether or not you realize it. Then your boss is reacting to those feelings without really understanding what's happening.

But here's the good news: YOU have the power to change the whole dynamic just by focusing on yourself and your feelings.

It might look like this:

- When my boss rolls his eyes at me, it makes me mad. How dare he treat a child like that?

- When my boss shouts for me to come into her office without looking up from her desk, it makes me feel worthless. How can she be so insensitive towards a child?

- My boss interrupts me and tries to finish my sentences even when he doesn't know what he's talking about. What a crummy way to support a child in sharing her opinion!

When your nervous system gets upset, it's in threat-response mode. Do you know how old you were when you developed your threat-response mode? You were a CHILD!

So when you're feeling angry, sad, upset or threatened, your boss IS talking to a child. He or she is talking to the child you were when your nervous system learned to negotiate that particular feeling. And because upset feelings in childhood so frequently relate to parents or parent-like figures, you are asking them to parent you without knowing it. Yikes!

What to Do Now?

Now that you have your list of the ways your boss triggers your childhood pain, your new job is to get daily nurturing for that childhood pain—but not from your boss! It could be by having a check-in call with a buddy in the morning to exchange the listening and nurturing that will help ensure your childhood pain (and maybe theirs too) stays in its rightful place during the workday.

(Ideally, your friend is also reading this book so they understand what you're up to—and perhaps they want to work on their own childhood pain.)

It could be by writing soothing affirmations to your inner child, telling her she is safe and loved.

It could be by writing a conversation between big you and little you where little you tells you everything she's scared of. And big you listens and comforts her.

It could be by meeting a friend for coffee in the morning before work.

It could be by inviting a friend at work to do a quick check-in in the bathroom at the start of the day. (Again, you might want to invite your colleague to read this book with you.)

I did all those things and more to shift my behavior around Owner-Boss-Lady.

More Nora Story: The Make-Or-Break Week

Please understand, I was so terrified, I was willing to do whatever it took to save my job. In part, this was because I couldn't see what was wrong with me. I was truly living in blind spots. Breaking through those blind spots into new awareness was often painful. But I knew I had to do it. My whole capacity to be a functional adult seemed to hang in the balance.

Because I had so many blind spots, I didn't understand WHY certain things worked and other things didn't. I didn't understand a lot of the things that ended up helping me heal and grow on my career journey. I just tried them because I was desperate. It was only much later that I came to understand why they worked.

First, I went back to that new job affirmation and realized I'd gotten exactly what I'd hoped for. My boss may not have been healthy or sane. But she sure was fascinating and interesting. I decided to change the affirmation to:

Thank you God for my healthy, sane, fascinating, high-paying, abundant job you send me with grace and ease.

This helped to shape my mindset a little. But I knew I needed some serious action changes to go with my thought changes.

Remember how Owner-Boss-Lady told me that I had a week to shape up or I'd be gone by Friday? Well, starting that Monday, I got up super-early and traveled more than an hour to a support group meeting at 7:30 in the morning. I spent that hour-long meeting listening to other people share about their crazy parents, crazy bosses, crazy spouses, and crazy kids.

I felt scared and uncomfortable, hearing all these people share such intimate feelings, but they seemed just fine with me talking about my own fears about my boss and my mother. When it wasn't my turn to share, I wrote affirmations to calm my nerves. I was a very nervous young woman that morning.

What I didn't realize at the time was that sitting in that meeting made a huge impact on my nervous system. Why? Because these people could give me the gentle listening, acceptance, love and emotional support I never got from my mom. These people could give my nervous system the safety it craved that my boss would never be able to give me.

At the time, I did not understand this at all. All I knew was that I felt different somehow—calmer—when I walked into work that Monday morning. Somehow, I managed not to show up as needy or over-emotional across the entire day, not even once. I started organizing my desk using some strategies suggested by friends who thought I might have a touch of ADHD. By some miracle, I got to the end of the day without any weird words from my boss. I felt like I had managed to pretend to be confident all day.

Something in me knew that I needed to go to another 7:30 support group meeting on Tuesday morning—that somehow the benefit of the Monday meeting would expire within 24 hours. Don't ask me how I knew this. I just knew it.

So I went again. And Tuesday was another pretend confidence day. I continued implementing new productivity strategies for follow-through and neatness and tried to get as much work done as I could.

That week, I went to a 7:30 support group meeting every morning. On Wednesday, Owner-Boss-Lady walked up to my newly color-coded, organized desk and said, "I can see you're really trying." I was so afraid of responding with my needy parent-seeking self. I wanted to say, "Really? Really? You see that I'm trying? Because I'm working so, so, so hard!!" But I knew that would set her off. So all I said was, "Um, thanks."

On Thursday, I found my first viable candidate for one of our executive searches. I had a great talk with her on the phone and then brought her résumé to Owner-Boss-Lady. Owner-Boss-Lady was actually interested and told me to schedule a call for the following morning.

The call with the new candidate on Friday morning went really well, and we set up a live interview for the following week. I scurried back to my office as soon as the call was over, terrified of seeming needy or exhibiting approval-seeking behavior to my boss.

On Friday afternoon, a miracle happened, Owner-Boss-Lady walked into the office I shared with a really smart, seasoned recruiter who became a mentor to me later. Let's call her Sally-Ann.

Owner-Boss-Lady stood in our doorway and practically sang:

"Who's the Most Valuable Player of the Week?"

I had never seen her like this. "Um, Sally-Ann?"

"No, Dummy, you!!"

The compliment came as a complete shock. I had been so focused on holding in all my neediness, it never occurred to me that my boss would actually enjoy approving of my good work (rather than my wounded soul).

Again, I didn't understand why things had shifted in my capacity to stay calm and appear self-sufficient at work, but I did understand that those morning support group meetings felt like some sort of magic. I resolved to go every weekday morning before work, no matter what. I just had the sense that if I did, I wouldn't be fired. I went to those 7:30 a.m. support group meetings every weekday for two years. And you know what? I never received a negative performance review from a boss ever again.

Back to Kathryn...

Are you impressed with my story? Well, Kathryn wasn't. She did like the story. She just didn't see how it applied to her and her relationship with her boss, Quentin.

So I told her **another** story.

Greta: How Do I Feel Right Now?

Greta was a rising star executive at a very fancy investment bank in New York. Her intellect and skills were well-respected by her team and by her superiors. She had built positive, friendly relationships across the organization.

Greta and her direct boss had had a terrific rapport for several years. She viewed their collaborations as one of the highlights of her job. They had even moved up the ladder together at least once—he to Senior Vice President, she to Vice President.

Everything would have been smooth sailing except...

In the previous few months, Greta had become deeply distressed about her relationship with her boss. Out of nowhere, Greta's boss had become a screamer.

She didn't quite know how to deal with his screaming. It was an entirely new phenomenon. Where she had once strode confidently into his office several times a day, she now found herself avoiding him and walking in on tip-toe only when she absolutely had to.

The tool I gave Greta was not about changing her behavior toward her boss. It was about changing her behavior toward herself. You see, Greta's childhood home was filled with raised voices, shouting and arguing. Greta hated it as a child and she hated it as an adult. It made her feel small and hopeless.

But Greta was no longer small and hopeless. "Greta," I explained to her, "when you were a child, you were a hostage. All children are hostages. Children can't speak up for themselves. They're vulnerable and dependent, so whatever happens, they just have to sit there, feeling small and hopeless. But that's not you.

"You, Greta, are an adult. You can always re-negotiate. You can always change your mind."

Greta liked that. She repeated it: "I'm an adult. *I can always re-negotiate. I can always change my mind.*"

"So, with this boss, whatever is in his private head that has suddenly become so painful that he's taking it out on everyone else—that's none of your concern. Your only job is to take very, very good care of yourself in a way no one ever taught you to take care of yourself."

"From now on, whenever this guy starts to raise his voice, all you have to say is: *I'm feeling uncomfortable with the way this conversation is going. I'm going to leave the room. And we can continue this at another time.*

"Please note, you don't blame him, judge him, fix him, or tell him what to do. It's not about him. It's about you taking care of your feelings and your well-being by gently excusing yourself if you become uncomfortable. That's all."

Greta responded, "I gotta be honest, Nora, what you're suggesting scares me but I LOVE it. Can we practice it a few times? Can you pretend to be my boss and get mean, raise your voice—and then I can practice saying it?"

I had already explained to Greta about how the nervous system creates new muscle memories by rehearsing healthy new tools like the one I had just given her. I was delighted to see her requesting a rehearsal before I even suggested it. After about three repetitions, she said she felt ready.

So when Greta went into that Monday morning, what do you think happened? How about I let Greta tell you...

"It was the weirdest thing, Nora. I got to work Monday morning, and for the first time in months, I was actually feeling excited to talk to my boss. I just couldn't wait to use my new tool. I'd been mentally rehearsing all weekend. It scared me to stick up for myself like that. But even just imagining myself saying it as I prepared over the weekend made me feel powerful and liberated."

"Around 10 a.m., I actually had a reason to talk to him, so I walked over to his office. I hesitated at the door and said my new mantra one more time in my head, ***I'm feeling uncomfortable with the way this conversation is going. I'm going to leave the room. And we can continue this at another time.***

"When I walked into his office and greeted him, I immediately had the thought, ***Do I feel uncomfortable right now?*** and a little voice in my head answered, ***No, you're fine, keep talking.***

"We started discussing what I had needed to discuss with him and I heard that thought again, ***How about now? Am I uncomfortable now? No. How about now? Still no.***

"Honestly, it was almost disappointing. I was looking forward to feeling all the courage and excitement I just knew I would feel when it was time to say my new line. But I just kept asking myself, ***How do I feel right now? How do I feel right now?*** And the answer was always—I feel just fine.

"HOWEVER, when I left the room, I realized it was the first time my boss hadn't yelled at me in months! And do you know he didn't yell at me for the rest of the week?

"Now, here's the crazy part—he was still yelling at other people but he absolutely did not yell at me. It was like once I knew that I could leave the room if I wanted to, I didn't have to say it out loud. Just having the knowledge that I wasn't a hostage, that I could leave the room at any time whenever I wanted to—having that knowledge made me feel confident and relaxed. It was like I was kryptonite to his yelling."

I was so proud. "Greta, that's fantastic. Truly amazing work! I can't read minds, but I wonder if the reason things shifted so quickly could be that your silent commitment to the deepest level of self-care brought a level of safety and peace into the room that he found soothing. Poor guy, he must be in a lot of pain."

It became clear a few months later that he **was** in a lot of pain when he was fired for mis-appropriating firm funds (fraud), and Greta was promoted to replace him. But do you know that for that entire time, even as her poor boss was falling apart at the seams and screaming at everyone, **HE NEVER YELLED AT GRETA EVER AGAIN.**

Tool: The Comfortable/Uncomfortable Game

Is your boss or someone in your life triggering a strong negative reaction in you?

What can you do to develop a tool like the one Greta found so useful?

Remember that the tool works best when it's all about you and your comfort level. Literally, all you have to do is ask yourself: Am I comfortable or uncomfortable right now?

No blame, shame or judgment of the other person. Just pure listening to yourself and your needs and being willing to **gently** make your needs your most important priority no matter what the other person is doing.

Honestly, that line I gave Greta works on just about any upsetting behavior with no shame or blame (as long as you don't use it to punish anyone or create a drama). Here it is again:

I'm feeling uncomfortable with the way this conversation is going. I'm going to leave the room. And we can continue this at another time.

How do you say it with minimal drama? The key is to say it quietly and gently but then follow through by firmly walking out of the room. It's like Theodore Roosevelt used to say, "Speak softly and carry a big stick."

If you're tempted to make a scene or show off your moral superiority, then you will have flipped into survival mode. And, once you're in survival mode, you'll be using this line to lash out at the saber-toothed tigers that aren't really in the room.

The only way this line works is if you use it as your reminder for yourself that you are safe and that your moment-to-moment feelings really do matter and deserve to be listened to, especially by you. That's a message very few of us received as children.

FYI, this process of listening to yourself and setting behavior-based limits that honor your own discomfort with NO blame and NO shame is one of the most effective ways to create healthy boundaries in any relationship. We'll talk more about this in later chapters.

[For more on the Comfortable/Uncomfortable Game, go to www.getaheadandstayahead.com.]

Back to Kathryn...

"OK, Nora, I like this story better but I'm still not sure it applies to my relationship with MY BOSS. I don't feel scared of Quentin when he yells. I'm just frustrated that we're not getting more done."

"Hmm," I said, "it sounds like you're a Confident Colleen."

"A Confident who?"

"Let me tell you the story of Fraidy Kat and Confident Colleen."

It Happens EVERYWHERE

As a consultant to more than 100 companies, I've seen countless boss/employee relationships with many different issues. But the scenario below is especially common. In fact, it's so common that it doesn't even make sense to give you a name and a location.

Imagine a script that goes something like this:

Fraidy Kat: Excuse me, pardon me, so sorry to interrupt, I just had the tiniest question.

Boss (yelling): JUST ASK THE QUESTION!

Fraidy Kat (even more scared now): Oh, I'm so sorry to bother you, and I see that perhaps now isn't the best time since it appears that perhaps I have interrupted you.

Boss (yelling louder): Oh My God!! Just ask me the damn question!!

Fraidy Kat (quivering with fear now): Oh dear, oh dear, oh dear, I was just wondering about the...you know what, I'll come back later. (She runs out.)

Then the Boss turns to me and says:

You see, Nora, they waste my time all day!!

When I talk to Fraidy Kat later, she says:

Nora, I'm so frustrated. It's just impossible to find him in a good mood so that I can ask a question without getting yelled at.

What **Fraidy Kat** doesn't know is that **Boss** was in a terrific mood before she walked in. But she's so afraid of being yelled at that she stumbles over her words and triggers the ONE thing that annoys him the most—feeling like his time is being wasted. In his mind, he raises his voice so that he can be heard over her time-wasting talk. And all he's asking her to do is be direct and get to the point. Why? BECAUSE HE ACTUALLY WANTS TO HELP HER!

Many bosses I've worked with fit this description perfectly. They actually say things to me about their employees like:

"All I want to do is help them, but none of them can ask me a simple question."

Or:

"I tell them to bring me the bottom line, and they bring me a bunch of unrelated details that have nothing to do with the question they need to answer."

Here's how that interaction would go if the employee could pretend to herself that she wasn't afraid of the boss:

Confident Colleen: Hey Jack, got a minute for a question about the Andrews account? (Note the immediate summary of context.)

Boss: What's up? (He's calm and efficient.)

Confident Colleen: Do we need to put the extra security controls in place before or after the developer puts the new codes in?

Boss: Mmm, good question. Can you call Jenna and ask her?

Confident Colleen: Do you think she'll know?

Boss: If she doesn't, then I'll call Barb and she can tell us, OK?

Confident Colleen: Sounds like a plan. (She walks out.)

Boss: Hey, thanks Colleen!

Confident Colleen (Calling over her shoulder): Don't mention it!

Wham-bam, thank you ma'am! Every boss I've observed these dynamics with has at least one Fraidy Kat and at least one Confident Colleen. It's not that Fraidy Kat doesn't want to get things done. And the boss never wants to scare poor Fraidy Kat. He's just stressed out and anxious about getting everything done. When the boss is stressed and anxious, he yells. When Fraidy Kat is scared, she apologizes and over-talks. Her over-talk heightens her boss's anxiety as the minutes tick by during her interruption without any real work being discussed.

The irony is that the Boss has a lot more in common with Fraidy Kat than with Confident Colleen. Confident Colleen keeps things professional and calm. In fact, both the Boss and Fraidy Kat often get the answers they need from Confident Colleen. If the Boss is the owner of the company, then Confident Colleen will become his right-hand person very quickly. If the Boss works for someone else, or in a big corporate structure, with the right tools, Confident Colleen could easily be promoted to the Boss's level or above.

Whenever I sit down with the Fraidy Kats of the world, I inevitably discover that in childhood they had a parent who yelled at them. Or no one ever yelled at them so they shut down in bewilderment.

When Fraidy Kat walks into the Boss's office, knowing she depends on him for resources, the first thing she's trying to assess is "Is it safe?" From the first time she ever heard him raise his voice, her antenna has been up for when it feels safe to talk with him and when it doesn't.

The kind of safety Fraidy Kat is looking for is what I call emotional security. It's definitely a great thing to learn from a parent. It's an impossible resource to get from a boss.

When Fraidy Kat looks to her Boss for safety and emotional security, she doesn't realize that she's asking him to take on the role of parent to her. Unfortunately, bosses usually don't have the time, knowledge or skill to give their employees the parenting they missed in childhood.

In my first four weeks with Owner-Boss-Lady, whenever I had a question for her, I was totally a Fraidy Kat. And I had never even heard her yell at that point! It's just that I was bringing all my childhood pain and fear to work with me every day. My traumatizing track record of being fired so often probably compounded my fear as well. So, without knowing it, I was over-talking and quivering and infusing my tone with drama and fear and neediness in ways that were driving poor Owner-Boss-Lady crazy!

Your Turn

Are you a Fraidy Kat or a Confident Colleen? Most of us are a little of both, depending on the situation.

Let's look at the parent/boss resource distinction again:

Ideally, parents give children:

- Food, water, shelter, clothing for nourishment and physical protection.
- Love, validation and approval for self-esteem.
- Attention, focus, care and healthy boundaries for a sense of self-care, independence and emotional security.
- Clear expectations, guidance and appropriate rewards and consequences for learning to negotiate the world.
- Wisdom and life lessons for how to succeed in the world.

Ideally, bosses give employees:

- Payment that allows them to purchase food, water, shelter, clothing, etc.
- Approval for a job well done.
- A clear mission, expectations and context for motivation and strategic thinking.
- Guidance for negotiating and achieving specific goals.
- Mentorship for personal and professional growth.

Are you asking your boss for things that are on the parent list?

Do you find that your boss falls short on the boss list?

When your boss falls short on the boss list, how do you feel?

Is it possible that your boss falling short on the boss list triggers your defensiveness without realizing it, and before you know it, you're asking for things on the parent list from your boss?

Does your boss ever do things that remind you of one parent or another?

Is it possible that when your boss reminds you of one of your parents, you start asking for things on the parent list without realizing it?

Kathryn Again...

"I really appreciate all these ideas, Nora, but I really am a Confident Colleen. At least I think I am. I love getting stuff done, I'm not terribly emotional, I don't take stuff personally, and I would love it if you could offer some tips on how to get my crazy boss into a better frame of mind so we can turbocharge!"

I may not have mentioned before that this series of conversations with Kathryn took place over quite a number of months. By this time in our relationship, I had a much better understanding of her, her boss Quentin, and the quirks of their relationship.

Here is what turned out to be the key to Kathryn's breakthrough.

Quentin was as jumpy and erratic as a bouncing rubber ball. Gregarious and happy one minute, frustrated and angry the next. He had a habit of asking for 10 different items, then forgetting he had asked for them and getting very upset and focused on something completely different—

which sent everyone in the office running. Then two or three weeks later he would throw a tantrum because item #6 from that original list of 10 was incomplete.

AND, Quentin would yell at Kathryn saying he had asked for it a dozen times when in fact, he'd asked for it once. To top it all off, most of the time, when work was incomplete, Quentin was the bottleneck. She would take action on all 10 items and then ask for certain information or guidance from him, which he might or might not supply, depending on his schedule, his mood, or his other priorities for the day.

Kathryn was a remarkably competent worker—flexible, resilient, easygoing and rigorous. She was a master of letting Quentin's nastiness roll off her back. But she had begun to have physical issues—acid reflux, nightmares, panic attacks. It was as though her body was rejecting the experience of working for her boss even when her mind was determined to be a great team player.

One day, months into my work with both of them, I sat them down in the conference room.

"Kathryn," I said, "I think there are two pieces of information about Quentin that will make a huge difference for you."

They both looked at me expectantly.

"First, on the emotional side: I think it's natural to experience moments when Quentin raises his voice or expresses frustration as…" I paused. This was a little risky to say. "I think it's natural to experience these moments as times when it feels like he's the master and you're the servant, and you have failed him again. And you feel like you're dirt beneath his feet." Kathryn looked like she was holding her breath. Quentin was looking more agitated every second.

"BUT I don't think that's what Quentin wants you to feel. And I certainly don't think that's what Quentin intends to communicate."

They relaxed a little.

"I want you to think of it this way. Quentin is a sports guy—he loves to play on teams—basketball, hockey, volleyball—he's in all those men's leagues, right, Quentin?" Quentin nodded.

"When he's on the volleyball court and his team misses an opportunity to score, he shouts in frustration—not because he's angry with his teammates, but because he cares so much about the team winning that he has to recognize and express his disappointment as the first step in helping the team step it up so they can win."

"That's so true, Nora," Quentin said, "I love to win as a team, and I'm gonna tell the truth and do whatever it takes to get us to win together. No matter what sport it is."

"I'm so glad to hear you say that, Quentin," I said. "Because I think Kathryn needs to understand that when you express frustration, you're expressing frustration about the situation to her as your teammate, not as someone inferior to you."

"Oh yeah," he said, "it's no fun to have people below me. I want people on my team running as hard as I run, caring as much as I care."

"Bingo!" I said. "Caring as much as Quentin cares. Kathryn, I think you can transform your experience AND Quentin's experience by expressing frustration with Quentin as though the two of you are equals and teammates. Because in his mind, you are equals."

"So, when Quentin says 'That sucks!' what do I say?" asked Kathryn.

"You say, 'yeah, it does suck! What are we gonna do about it?'"

"Huh," said Kathryn. "Will that work?"

"That actually sounds pretty good to me," said Quentin.

"I'm glad that you like it, Quentin, but Kathryn needs to remember that it won't always work because sometimes your frustration will be too big…can you confirm that?"

"It's not something I'm excited about, but, yes, I know sometimes I just can't shake how frustrated I feel."

"This leads me to the second tool," I said.

"Kathryn, you and Quentin have a number of structures that are designed to keep projects as organized as possible, right?"

"Oh sure," said Kathryn, "morning meetings, afternoon check-ins, weekly numbers meetings, you name it."

"And how often does Quentin miss your appointments?"

"About 30 to 40% of the time, I think," said Kathryn.

"From what Quentin tells me, I think it's 60 to 70%."

"Really? Are we that bad?"

"I'm the worst," said Quentin.

"OK, OK, so we can acknowledge that Quentin missing meetings slows down work-flow. But Kathryn, here's the kicker: When Quentin misses a meeting, you think you're being nice by not nagging him about meetings he misses. But in his mind, unless he hears from you that you are in the office and ready for the meeting, he assumes you forgot too."

"I just don't want to put any more pressure on him."

"But that's the thing. He doesn't see it as pressure. He sees it as you being reliable so that he can go off and be a mess. He needs you to be that safe structure that's always there, no matter what he's doing, so that he can be free to be spontaneous with clients, ideas, time, whatever."

"AND," said Quentin, "if you email me to say that you're sitting at your desk waiting for our morning meeting, even if I can't make it, at least I know you're available for specific requests from me. I know you're great about checking your phone at night. But I actually try not to bother you until I know you're in the office."

"And he doesn't know you're in the office if you're 'protecting him from pressure.' For him, if he doesn't know you're here, he assumes you're unreliable and that he's the more reliable one—

"Which scares me," said Quentin, "because I know how unreliable I am."

"And when people are scared, they get defensive, they yell, they get upset," I said.

"So you want me to email you that I'm ready to go for every meeting that you miss?" asked Kathryn.

"Yes!" said Quentin.

Then I added, "Just don't be passive-aggressive. Be positive, business-like, and unceasingly rigorous. Never miss a meeting. Never miss emailing him to let him know you're present when he's missing the meeting."

"Would that make you feel safe, Quentin?"

"So safe," he said, "so safe."

And sure enough, as Kathryn adopted our suggestions, things started to shift in the office.

Tool: Your Boss Is More Afraid of You

What if your boss feels lonely and scared?

Lonely in his frustration when things go off the rails.

Scared when employees don't show up the way she hopes and expects them to.

How can you start relating to your boss like the two of you are both playing for the same team?

Can you try taking negative things your boss says as a reflection of her commitment to making the whole team better?

Can you mirror her frustrating emotions in a supportive, teammate kind of way?

When your boss misses commitments to you, can you remind him that you're ready to work and take instruction however he can offer it, even if he has an unpredictable conflict with the commitment?

Labels Don't Make Friends

I've given you a number of tools that can help with all sorts of boss problems. But do you know what the biggest block to using these tools will be? Labels. What do I mean by labels? I mean the words your brain uses to describe your boss's negative qualities. As long as you're regularly labeling your boss's negative qualities, your perceptions will continue gathering evidence that your boss will never change and you will continue to see the source of your discomfort as firmly **OVER THERE.**

Remember how our nervous systems are always looking for threats? Well, they don't just identify threats, they assess them. Is this a saber-toothed tiger or a bobcat? Is that a wolf or a dog? Should I run away or hide in the bushes?

In order to assess danger, our brains and nerves constantly have to seek information about dangerous things around us. You are pre-programmed to experience uncomfortable experiences as a trigger for analysis and assessment so that you can "know your threat."

Sometimes that means your brain automatically generates labels in your head for difficult people. Labels like *crazy, mean, thoughtless, abusive, cruel, rude, manipulative, angry, moody*...you name it.

I'm not saying that your experience is wrong or invalid. Remember, honoring your feelings is very important in this process. And just so you know, your feelings are very important to me because I know for a fact that you (yes, YOU!) are an incredibly valuable person deserving of huge amounts of love, support, success, fun and joy.

When dealing with a difficult boss, your feelings might often include fear, sadness, shame, even guilt. You get to have as much support and listening for those feelings as you want from that tribe you keep building.

Your feelings are great. But your thoughts are a different story. If your thoughts insist on analyzing and labeling all the things your boss does wrong, it will be hard to implement the tools I've offered you in this chapter.

Instead of labeling your boss's behavior as crazy, manipulative, micro-managing, etc., try seeking to understand what's happening for him or her emotionally when you experience their difficult behavior.

Most of the time, your boss's difficult behavior is motivated by fear—fear that projects won't get done; fear that time and money will be wasted; fear that he or she is the only one keeping things together.

Every time your brain tells you to label your boss, you have an opportunity to get curious—curious about the growth that's possible inside you, the growth that's possible in your relationship with your boss, the growth that's possible in your ability to gain new skills, gain new understandings, and be more productive, more peaceful, more profitable, and more powerful.

[For more on transforming your nervous system's automatic labeling into tools that can help bring new levels of peace and harmony to your relationship with your boss, go to www.getaheadandstayahead.com.]

Lie #6: I Have to Be Perfect to Succeed

<u>Samantha's Story: I Can Start Once I'm Finished.</u>

"But Nora, I don't think I have to be perfect," Samantha told me, "just better than I am now."

Samantha was a personal organizer in an East Coast city who had steadily built a client following over several years. She hired me to help her grow large enough so that she could quit her full-time job and focus exclusively on her organizing business.

When we began working together, she was feeling totally stuck in the "what to do next" disease over how to grow her business and find more clients.

"Should I buy a bunch of giveaways with my logo on them? Should I pay someone to re-design my website? Should I re-decorate my office so I can impress high-end clients?"

To help her answer these questions, we made a prioritized list of actions that would grow her revenue most quickly. It was a useful exercise for her.

Sitting in front of the list of the ranked items, Samantha estimated the cost of each one.

"These prices seem really high, Samantha," I told her.

"But Nora, I need to have the best possible version of each item."

Looking at her budget, there was no way Samantha could afford the best possible version of each item.

"Samantha," I said, "is it possible that you could start with a less expensive version of some of these items and upgrade to the more deluxe versions over time as your revenue grows?"

"Oh no, Nora, it would make me completely crazy to do that. Everything has to look perfect with these particular items. I'll go nuts if it doesn't."

"Samantha," I said, "Having a deep internal drive to make things organized and orderly is part of what makes you terrific at being a personal organizer. But is it possible that your commitment to beauty is blocking your ability to allow your business to grow in the messy way that growth usually happens?"

"Messy? I hate that word."

We laughed.

"Growth is usually messy," I said. "You try one thing, it doesn't work, you toss it out and try something else. That works for two days then it breaks. Then you try something that fixes half your problem, but it turns out to be all you need for six months and then suddenly you have to fix the other half in three days. I know it sounds whacky. But that's what figuring out growth as we grow tends to look like.

"I know I must sound weird when I say that I want to grow perfectly, Nora. I guess I just wonder: if I make mistakes, won't that mean I'm failing?"

"Samantha," I said, "I started a total of four businesses within about two years. Only one of them became successful...the one where I use neuroscience to help people and companies grow. Now, that one is very successful, and I've worked with thousands of people and over 100 companies in 40 different industries, but I make mistakes all the time!"

"You do?"

"Oh sure, I've had clients tell me they hate me. I've had clients tell me that talking to me made them go home and cry for hours. I've had clients threaten to call 911 if I didn't get out of their office."

"Those don't sound like mistakes, those sound like moments when you were talking to crazy people."

"Well, growth can make people very scared and uncomfortable. And sometimes, their nervous systems tell them that I'm the source of their discomfort. I try not to take it personally, but it's so important for me to look at my behavior, apologize and put right anything I did do wrong. I like to believe that most of my mistakes are unintentional, so that means I'm going to be a little surprised when they happen."

"And scared, right?"

"Oh sure, it's always scary to find out that something I thought I was doing in a good way was painful or wrong for another person."

"So what do you do?"

"I say: Thank you so much for telling me. Please tell me more so that I can understand how to do better."

"And they tell you?"

"Most of the time, yes. But I've also been training them to tell me this kind of stuff from the beginning. You remember that little speech I gave you when we first started working together about loving it when you interrupt me, disagree with me, tell me I'm crazy..."

"Oh yeah..."

"Well, I learned to give that speech by making lots of mistakes and offending lots of people. It used to bum me out SO MUCH when I found out I had offended someone. But now..."

"But now, you always say that thing—what is it—often wrong?"

"Often wrong, rarely in doubt. That's me!"

We laughed again.

"Yeah, it doesn't have to be such a tragedy to have flaws. I mean I don't just make mistakes—I actually have character traits that come out and bite me in the butt."

"Like what?"

"Like being arrogant, condescending, melodramatic, needy, selfish, passive-aggressive."

"I don't experience you that way."

"And I'm so glad to hear it. But if you ever do experience any of those things from me, I want you to know that I'll be glad if you let me know."

"How can you be so calm about it?" Samantha asked.

"The truth is, Samantha," I said, "when I started embracing my mistakes and inviting criticism, I knew it was a good growth opportunity for me personally. But what really surprised me was that when I stayed calm and humble about my flaws and apologized without being dramatic or needy, it seemed to make my clients feel safer."

"Because they saw that if it was OK for you to be flawed and clean up your mistakes then it could be OK for them too."

"Bingo! Wow, that was a great way to say it, Samantha."

"That's because it's what I feel right now."

"I'm glad."

"But Nora, what about making mistakes with all these things I want to buy?"

"My rule of thumb is that I never take an untested financial risk unless I can afford to be wrong. So many things *look* like they might help grow the business. But the only way I know for sure is if that money I spend leads to new income. If it doesn't, then I've just purchased a new lesson in business learning—but I haven't gone broke doing it."

"Is that why you want me to try smaller-scale versions of my wish list items?"

"Yes, exactly, I want you to have the freedom to fail and learn from your failures without too much hanging in the balance."

"But Nora, if perfection is no longer my goal, how will I know when I've succeeded?"

"I believe that success is about achieving great results with integrity and fun. So many people suffer through their success or suffer through their procrastination and fear around actions that lead to success."

"So what's the secret to fun, imperfect success?"

"Releasing perfection for fun, imperfect success doesn't mean that we stop being ambitious or rigorous. It means that we find new ways to make our moment-to-moment experience of work pleasurable and stimulating as we grow and learn. And it just so happens that I've got some tools up my sleeve."

Trading Perfection for Customized Fun

Back when I was doing everything I could to avoid getting fired by Owner-Boss-Lady, I began to do a lot of reading on brain patterns related to focus, distraction and organization. As I researched the connections between these experiences, I started to understand just how differently human brains respond to different stimuli.

It seems obvious, doesn't it? Some of us get really excited for pretty colors. Others for wacky games. Still others go gaga for numbers and all the fun you can have with them. And others are wild for writing poetry or going to the theater or reading double-blind clinical studies.

We do this for kids. We create playgrounds and classrooms with all sorts of colors, sounds, smells, and textures. The best learning, we hear these days, gets kids into an experience. Don't just read about wave patterns, observe them at the beach. Don't just memorize facts about mammals, care for them at the local zoo.

Why do we think adults would be so different? When Owner-Boss-Lady called me disorganized, it was because I was struggling to keep my desk clean and keep track of my work. Sure, I wasn't procrastinating on tasks themselves (no personal email, internet or phone calls one day at a time). But I didn't have a structure or a system to organize and prioritize my work.

I knew I *should* have had a system. I knew I *should* have been the master of my work domain, but God help me if I knew how. My boring, ugly office desk, the overwhelming pile of papers. Those words—organized, system, structure—they all sounded so miserable and lifeless to me.

I used to "*should* on myself" a lot. In fact, I had a list of *shoulds* that I knew would be the ticket to perfection if I could only get myself to do them.

I used to think that with the right motivation at work, I would be motivated to do the **shoulds** that would make me perfect. But even when I had jobs where I felt motivated by the mission, the environment, or both, my moment-to-moment experience was very up and down. The truth was no matter what the big picture stuff was, if the little moments didn't feel good, then I was going avoid them.

Owner-Boss-Lady was mad at me because my desk was a mess. But I hated cleaning it because it didn't feel good to clean it. I loved talking to executives on the phone. I loved writing about them in candidate reports for our job searches. It had become easy to do these things even though they were new to me because I enjoyed doing them. But I was still at the level where anything that didn't naturally bring me a certain level of good feeling was just much harder to do.

I know what you're thinking—the 3-minute bridge! And you'd be right. But I didn't understand yet how the 3-minute bridge applied to getting organized at that point in my growth. The 3-minute bridge was something I learned to use for starting tasks. But putting things into a physical system felt like a much bigger issue.

Owner-Boss-Lady was crystal clear with me though, God bless her. Have an organized, clean desk or get fired. She was one of the biggest catalysts for growth I've ever encountered. I will be forever grateful to her.

Designing My Play-Desk

As I read more about different kinds of focus and distraction issues, I realized that I needed to create a playground at work for the child in me. I deserved to feel happy, creative and stimulated in as many moments as possible at work. And those moments weren't about the big picture or the most perfect me, they were about **breaking things down into the tiniest units possible**.

When I got to work on Monday morning of Make-or-Break Week, I immediately started turning my desk into a little wonderland of silliness, joy and delight just for me.

Prior to this moment, my desk had been a mess of piles. Piles of names and numbers to call. Piles of résumés to review. Piles of summary forms that Owner-Boss-Lady required that we fill out as we took down candidate job histories.

Now I needed to create a filing system. A friend had suggested multi-colored file folders. I was so desperate for any little action that made me feel like I was upping my chances of keeping my job. So my first action was to ask the office assistant to order multi-colored file folders for me.

Because it would take a few days for them to arrive, I found some multi-colored Post-its and cut them into colorful labels for the boring one-color manila folders I had found in the supply closet.

Then I taped tiny little colorful notes and pictures and doodles all around my desk, especially in the file drawers. I was trying to make all my most tedious, soul-sucking tasks as silly and fun as possible. I was so desperate to feel like I was doing something productive.

I know this sounds detailed and trivial, but it was incredibly transformative for me to create a clean, stimulating, fun place to file my papers, track follow-through actions, sort résumés and attend to the sifting and sorting that simply didn't come naturally to me.

40 Calls a Day

Then, I decided, I needed a way to track my calls each day. Owner-Boss-Lady told us multiple times: "You should all be making 40 calls a day." I heard this morning, noon and night from her. But she never did anything but talk about it. There was no reporting procedure for counting our 40 calls each day. There was just her outrage that none of us were as hard-working as she had been when she was a young recruiter.

Now as a consultant to more than 100 companies, I often help teams establish tracking systems and accountability structures to improve productivity. Just like a lot of the CEOs and managers I work with now, Owner-Boss-Lady knew that 40 calls per day was a good idea. But she had no idea how to train people to be accountable for doing them.

Instead, she fell victim to what so many bosses I work with today do with their teams. She told us what we should do and tried to make us feel guilty and ashamed for not doing it. But she never showed us how to follow her directions, and she never helped us figure out the ways we could each perform at our best.

I would find out later that most people who worked for Owner-Boss-Lady simply did whatever they imagined they were supposed to do until she fired them or they quit (mostly they quit). In fact, when I eventually did leave, I was the 33rd person to leave in two years. The company only had eight employees.

But Owner-Boss-Lady's shortcomings as a manager combined with my desperation to avoid getting fired meant that I was forced to learn to manage myself in a way that would serve me (and my future clients) for the rest of my life.

The Post-it Game

All I intended to do to track my calls was to pick a different color Post-it every day and draw the four sticks with a line through them, one at a time, till I reached 40 each day. I wanted it to look something like this:

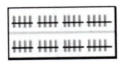

Except something happened on that Make-or-Break Monday. As I got to 30 calls by about 2 p.m., a little competitive voice in my head said, "Can you get to 40 by 3 p.m.?" Suddenly, my pace picked up and sure enough, I was at 40 by 2:56 p.m.

Then that same little voice said, "How about 50 calls by 4 p.m.?" And I was off to the races. Because I actually had high-quality conversations with a few new candidates in the final two hours, I couldn't go as fast as I had earlier in the day. But I proudly finished 52 calls by 5:30 p.m.

I dared not share my pride with Owner-Boss-Lady. I knew she would see it as approval-seeking and needy. And so I was forced to keep my joy to myself at work. But I did share my deliciously exciting, utterly simple game with my tribe friends. They told me it was great.

I played that game every day for the next nine months.

Within five months, I got promoted again AND I had the highest candidate placement rate of anyone in the firm.

Actions for Focus, Results for Learning

Owner-Boss-Lady had another mantra: "2 candidates a week." This meant that she wanted us to find at least 2 great candidates for our searches every week.

I tried focusing on that goal too. But, honestly, it didn't work for me. Some weeks I got zero candidates. Other weeks I got three or five. Those results came from at least 40 calls per day, day in, day out.

When I focused on results, I got worried and distracted. It was harder to focus on being of service to the person I was actually talking to in the present moment. When I focused on actions, everything flowed.

Sometimes, when I got caught up in results, I'd get annoyed that I had spent 25 minutes on the phone with a potential candidate who turned out to be wrong for a search at the very end. But the only way to cure my upset was to remember that the recruiter with the **most** No-candidates is ALSO the one with the **most** Yes-candidates.

Many people I work with now, especially people in sales, are terrified of wasting their time or hearing the word "no." For them, one "no" feels crummy. Five "no's" is clinical depression.

What they don't realize is that everyone is a "no" until they're a "yes" for just about everything in life. And each "no" is still a person with knowledge, ideas, and connections of their own. If you can treat the "no-people" with the same honor and sweetness that you treat the "yes-people," many no-people will be resources in other ways. Or they'll just be another "no" to add to your huge "no" pile that always helps bring more "yeses."

Is it ever useful to examine your results rates? Of course. But that examination is for learning and growing in your technique—not attempting to control outcomes.

When I was two years into recruiting, I had figured out a lot of useful strategies for efficiency that I had no clue about when I was only six months in. But when I was six months in, it didn't matter. What mattered was focusing on actions every day. In fact, by focusing on actions, I racked up results that could teach me how to be a better recruiter over time.

Discovering Mini-Units

These may seem like silly, minor things that I changed to increase my productivity. But in the years since, I've done SO MUCH MORE research and experimentation with these ideas.

What I've found in working with thousands of people and over 100 companies is that the way we have been trained to think about work and the way our bodies physically execute tasks are two completely different things.

We think about work in units of tasks, projects, goals, jobs, successes, failures, yes-people, no-people, salaries, bonuses, lay-offs, cuts, industries, life purposes, etc.

But we physically execute work in the tiniest moments strung together over time.

These moments involve very simple, granular actions. Let me give you a few examples:

Open document
Place fingers on keyboard
Start moving fingers

Or

Pick up telephone
Dial number
Listen to someone pick up and say "Hello"
Inhale
Start moving lips

A lot of us spend huge amounts of time thinking (and thinking and thinking) about the task, goal, success, failure, meaning or lack thereof before we actually place "fingers on keyboard" or "fingers on phone buttons" and begin.

In other words, to get stuff done, **no matter what our thoughts, plans or feelings,** if certain actions don't take place, then work is delayed.

But you know what happens? We think about the task, the project, the goal, the unknown variables (a.k.a. saber-toothed tigers). We think about failure, success, disappointment, frustration, "what ifs," and "what will they say ifs."

We rarely think about the fact that:

1) The work itself is made up of these tiny physical mini-units (like "fingers on keyboard" and "fingers on phone buttons").

2) All we need is something to make our fingers feel good. Everything else will either be a problem we'll negotiate with our imperfect tools when it arrives or a fantasy we've made up that will never actually happen.

Make Fingers Happy

What if our only job at work is to make our fingers feel safe and good enough to put themselves to work?

You think I'm being silly. But let's think about another activity people invest a lot of meaning in: sleep.

Can you imagine if you judged and assessed how many hours of sleep you got per week and per month but you never thought about the actual comfort of your bed? Can you imagine if you never bought a mattress you liked, or found nice-feeling sheets, or used any pillows?

We all know and accept that everybody needs a little something different in order to get a good night's rest. Some people like lots of pillows. Some people like just one. Some people like to sleep in a cold room with lots of blankets. Some people like to sleep in a warm room with no blankets.

Hopefully, we've all learned to care about the "head on pillow" experience (like "fingers on keyboard") because it has enormous influence over how much and how well we will sleep, one night at a time.

But can you imagine if you thought like this...

- Sleep is sleep is sleep.

- It shouldn't matter if you're sleeping on a wooden floor or a concrete slab or bed of hay.

- You get sleep done because it is what you do.

- You get sleep done because it is virtuous to sleep and sinful to stay up all night.

- You get sleep done whether you like it or not because otherwise you will be a worthless insomniac.

Pretty silly, right?

But this is how many of us think about work. Look at what happens if I put work-related words into those same bullet points...

- Work is work is work.

- It shouldn't matter if you're working at a big desk or a tiny table or in a windowless office.

- You get work done because it is what you do.

- You get work done because it is virtuous to work and sinful to procrastinate.

- You get work done whether you like it or not because otherwise you will be a worthless lazy bum.

Look, I've tried to live like this about work. It was certainly the way I believed work was for a very long time. And it didn't get me very far.

Remember, getting fired all those times?

Building a Mini-Unit Playground

Sleep is about relaxation and work is about engagement. For sleep, we build a comfortable bed for your body. For work, we build an engaging playground for your fingers, your eyes, your ears, and your heart.

The idea is to bring pleasure to the mini-units of your work activities so that you are energized and stimulated without being distracted or diverted.

For me, I needed pretty colors to engage me around filing and organizing.

And, I needed fun, silly games and competitions with myself (and with others) to stimulate my hunger to "go for it" with large numbers of repetitive tasks (cold calls).

What else did I need? I needed to feel meaningful and purposeful in my tiniest actions. So with each cold call, I said a little prayer to create a positive experience for the person on the other end of the line. My goal was to have them feel listened to and celebrated, regardless of whether they were right for the search I was working on or not.

Discovering My Most Important Mini-Unit Need

Why was having people feel good about my recruiting calls to them so important to me? Because when Owner-Boss-Lady would train me by having me listen in on her recruiting calls, I could tell when she would decide the candidate wasn't good enough for the search. Here was the problem: the candidate could tell too. Within a short time, both Owner-Boss-Lady and the person on the phone were swimming in antagonism and defensiveness. Finally, she would get them off the phone, roll her eyes and say, "What a stinker!"

I knew if I made people feel bad about themselves on cold calls, I would never, ever be able to do this job.

So I invented a new model for myself. I called it the "Tell Me Model." After exchanging pleasant greetings, I would give an impressive, sexy bite of information that would pique the candidate's interest long enough to keep them on the phone. Something like: "We're recruiting senior positions for one of the top five private equity firms in the country."

Then I'd say, "But before I go on, would you like to know a little about my firm, just so you know who you're talking to?" Of course they'd say yes...these first two questions matched Owner-Boss-Lady's script. But then I got creative.

When I finished my two sentences about the firm, I'd say, "But enough about me, tell me about you, tell me your career vision, and let me see if I can help you. Where are you from originally?"

And then I would ask them lots of questions about themselves and be sure to respond to all sorts of details with relatability and compliments. Things like, "Oh you're from Georgia? I'm from Louisiana! I love Atlanta. Was your town near Atlanta?"

Or, "Oh, you went to Stanford, were you there when Chelsea Clinton was there? What was THAT like?"

Or, "Wow, you were a Baker Scholar at Harvard Business School? You must have been a real idiot. Would you get it together already?" Then they would laugh.

Each tiny mini-unit of conversation became a delight because I looked for ways to make it delightful. I looked for ways to feel good by making them feel good.

And once I'd heard their life story, I could tell them if I thought they might be right for a search and start talking about the job.

If I knew they were wrong for the search, I could say, "Now tell me, what should I be keeping in mind for you?" Then I'd say, "I don't have that right now but could you please send me your résumé so that we can keep in touch? Also, here's all my info. Please reach out to me for anything—feedback on your résumé, work dynamics, you name it."

Isn't that hilarious? Crazy, multiple-times-fired ME offering to help some of the most successful executives in the country with THEIR work-dynamic issues? But most of them actually seemed to think I could help them.

Then, I'd say, "Would you like to hear about the searches I'm working on just to get a sense of how the job market looks these days?" They'd almost always say yes. And the ones who said no tended to be the least savvy folks.

Then, I'd tell them about the searches I was working on. If I had a search close to what they said they wanted, and I knew they weren't a good candidate, I would emphasize something outside their control as the reason it wasn't a good fit (so they didn't feel insulted) and then ask if they knew anyone I should talk to about it. Sometimes people drew a blank. But more often than not, I got at least one or two referrals. Sometimes five or six. One fellow even gave me the names of 12 people to call. Twelve!

Within a short time, I was the referral queen (which always means faster candidate catching in the recruiting world).

Beauty and fun were very nice for my playground. But if I didn't feel as though I was making people feel good in as many mini-unit moments as possible on each cold call, then I could not do my work.

Tool: Build Your Mini-Unit Playground

What are some overwhelming tasks you can turn into mini-units?

What can you do to make those mini-units fun for you no matter how tedious they seem?

Can you add music, pretty colors, fun images?

Can you add human connection, camaraderie, support?

Can you add opportunities to be kind to others, to take pleasure in being of service?

Can you make it silly, funny, fun and still get it done?

People do stuff they like doing. You are people. That means you.

People **pay attention** to stuff they like doing. You are people. That means you.

I want you to feel stimulated and happy in the tiniest, most granular units of your work. Then anticipating the big outcomes won't feel as scary because you'll be too focused on the moments that matter—the ones that are happening right now...and now...and now.

Focusing on making the little actions fun, motivating, and rigorous is part of what makes big achievements come a whole lot more quickly. And because you're narrowing your scope to the tiniest units, the perfectionism hiding in your nervous system has a lot less to say about how you dial a phone number than about how masterful you are in bending the outcome of the call to your perfect plan.

I've worked with a lot of companies whose leaders thought that bringing in a Ping-Pong table or taking everyone bowling was the way to create fun work. It's nice to blow off steam in a Ping-Pong game. And it's great when teams create camaraderie outside work hours. But the number one key to productivity is finding ways to make the work itself engaging and worthwhile for people while they're doing it.

[For more fun tips, tricks, and tools to create work that feels like play, go to www.getaheadandstayahead.com.]

I Can't Make Myself Do This

Occasionally, there's no amount of music, color or fun that makes a task easier.

Occasionally, a task is completely overwhelming no matter what we try.

At a certain point, we have to admit: We just can't. We just don't have the power to control ourselves as much as we thought.

When I figured out that no matter how much I tried, there were certain actions I was never going to be able to do, I actually sighed a big sigh of relief.

Why? Because the moment I accepted that I could not force myself to take action, I realized that there was another word that came at the end of that sentence.

So instead of: I just can't do this.

The sentence was: I just can't do this *alone.*

Once I knew I couldn't do something alone, all I had to do was ask for help.

It was humbling to call my friend Sheldon and say, "I just can't make myself open this online bank account. Will you stay on the phone with me while I do it?"

Luckily, I have great friends. "Of course, Nora," said Sheldon, "Shall I tell you about the sunset I can see from my window while you do it?"

So Sheldon started to tell me about the sunset as I began slowly following the directions to open my first online bank account.

At a certain point, I passed my 3-minute bridge and transitioned from the anxiety of STARTING to the excitement of DOING. Sheldon's soothing words went from being calming to being annoying.

"Sheldon," I said as politely as I could, "I'm really trying to focus on my online banking right now. Could I call you later and talk about the sunset then?"

"Victory!" Sheldon declared. "You don't even have to call me back."

Sheldon and I had that conversation many years ago but I still use this tool all the time. Sometimes, people I call don't even know I'm using it on them. I'll call them up, ask how they are and then work on a spreadsheet I've been avoiding as I listen to them tell me about whatever is going on for them. I'll usually clue them in by saying...

"Do you mind if I do some work I've been avoiding while we talk? It would help me so much to have your company over the phone, and I think it's mindless enough that I can give you *most* of my attention. But if I lose track of something you're saying because I get too absorbed, can you help me catch up in the conversation without getting upset with me?"

Because I lay it out as honestly and humbly as I can, people usually don't get upset with me over this issue.

Every time I grow, there's a chance that taking an action I've never taken before will fall into the "I can't do it alone" category. In fact, sometimes new actions are so scary, I need company in person.

For instance, writing this book with so many very personal stories, so many client stories from years of work, and such a huge desire to deliver value to you (yes, YOU!) has been a terrifying action for me. I've surrounded myself with supportive friends on the phone and in person. In fact, I wrote the first 60 pages with at least one other person in the room with me, punctuated by check-in calls to others.

When the stakes are high and the tasks are new, my nervous system sees saber-toothed tigers everywhere. So I need lots of other people in my tribe to keep me company and help me feel safe.

Marcia's Story: But I Just Can't!

Marcia was an accountant from Ohio who was visiting her best friend in New York when we met. Our work on her business was mostly over the phone.

One day, she called me from Texas, where she was on vacation with her husband and son.

"Nora, I know I committed to sending those five emails when we last talked, but I'm on vacation and I just can't!"

"Marcia, I hear you that it feels like that, but I don't think that's actually the case."

"No, you see, I can't sit down to work because what if my son needs me?"

"What if he does? You'll either ask him to wait a few minutes or you'll interrupt your work and come back to it."

"But what if our friends see me working on vacation? Won't they feel snubbed? Or won't they think I'm terrible for working on my vacation?"

"Why do they have to know?"

"Do you want me to LIE?"

"If they ask you directly, by all means tell them, but what does it matter to them what you do in your private time?"

"Well, that's just it, with everything going on, I have NO PRIVATE TIME!"

"Really? Where are you right now?"

"In one of the bedrooms in the house where we're staying."

"And are you surrounded by people?"

"No."

"So if you can take the time to call me in your private time, couldn't you take the time to do a little work?"

"But I..."

"Marcia, do you not want to work on your vacation? That's a perfectly legitimate choice that people make. You can just decide to work when you get back."

"NO, I really do want to send these emails."

"But maybe you can't."

"What?"

(She was not expecting me to co-sign her self-defeating attitude...oh, reverse psychology can be so much fun!)

"Maybe you can't make yourself send the emails alone, but you could if you got help. Would you like to send the emails with me on the phone?"

"Now? Right now? Without even asking permission?"

"Marcia, did you ask permission when you went to the bathroom today?"

"No."

"Have you taken any naps this week?"

"I took one today."

"Did you ask permission to do that?"

"No, I just did it."

"So can you just send these emails with me on the phone right now and not worry about what other people are secretly thinking? Truth be told, I don't think your friends or family members are that worried about time you're not spending with them right now."

"You're right! You're riiiiiiight! Why am I so obsessed with what other people think of me?"

"Maybe your nervous system thinks it's safer to believe that other people don't want you to work than to admit that for whatever reason, you just can't make yourself send these emails. But you don't have to force yourself to do something you can't do alone. All you have to do is ask for help."

"OK, I'm turning on my laptop as we speak. Wow, Nora, you were right, I feel horrible and terrified right now. I don't think I'd be able to do this without you on the phone."

"That's why human connection and safety are so important when we're taking scary actions. You're doing great. Keep going..."

And sure enough, Marcia sent all those emails.

Marcia's fear that she needed permission from other people or needed to do her work "in the perfect way" was part of the perfectionism that keeps us from taking action. Remember, these lies our nervous systems tell us are designed to keep us in survival, not growth. The more we obsess about being perfect, the less likely we are to take a risk or experiment with something that could drive us forward into success.

Tool: Use Your Tribe (Don't Do It Alone!)

Where is your brain/nervous system giving you reasons why you can't do something that's within your physical capabilities?

Do those reasons have to do with what people think of you?

With what might happen if you fail?

With what might happen if you get rejected?

With what might happen if you're not perfect?

With what might happen if doing it causes you pain?

What if no matter what the thoughts are in your head...what if the only reason you can't do it is that you can't do it alone?

Are you willing to call a buddy and ask them to keep you company so that you don't have to do it alone?

Are you aware that they will probably be inspired by your courage and moved by your vulnerability?

Perfectionism is the number one way we procrastinate. Can you allow yourself to receive the help you deserve to break through the scary perfectionist thoughts right now?

Now, are you doing it? Are you doing it right now? If not now, when?

[For more support on using your tribe and bursting through the "I can't do it alone" moments we all have, visit www.getaheadandstayahead.com.]

Lie #7: I Can't Ask for What I Want

So many of us have trouble believing that it's OK to ask for what we want. In fact, most of us have been told since we were very small that what we wanted was too much.

Remember Danielle, the composer I wrote about in the Introduction? When she was a child, her mother raged at her requests for simple things like food, clothes, and pocket change for school trips. Her father brought debilitating anxiety to the same issues. Her brain and nervous system interpreted those experiences and told her that it was dangerous to ask for what she wanted. In her case, the most obvious trigger for this sense of danger was asking for money. However, she didn't feel good asking for other things she wanted either.

A Nora Story: Am I Under-Earning?

So there I was, going to support group meetings every morning, writing affirmations, praying to be of service and ROCKING my Post-it game to make AT LEAST 40 calls a day. Oh, that Post-it game was so much fun. I still miss it.

Because of my success rate, I interviewed many more potential candidates than anyone else. These were amazingly intelligent senior corporate executives and senior management consultants from some of the largest and most powerful firms in the world.

As I watched them parade through our office in their crisp suits and freshly shined shoes, I became more and more self-conscious about the little underarm holes in my blouses. If I wanted to take off my jacket (the only one I owned), then I had to keep my arms as close to my body as possible.

It was hard to talk about, but eventually I was able to bring up the holes in my blouse to friends in my support groups. "Sounds like it's time to go shopping for new clothes, Nora!" a friend would say with enthusiasm. That was all well and good for her. A lot of them loved to bury their feelings in shopping. I was the opposite. Deprivation was where I felt safe. Going to stores gave me panic attacks.

Having threadbare clothes was a normal feature of childhood for me. Even though it felt humiliating when the other kids would notice my fraying clothes or the holes in my shoes, wearing those clothes was so much better than going shopping with my mom. Her screaming at me for being fat, ugly and disgusting in the middle of a department store dressing room had taught me long ago that shopping was a dangerous activity for me in childhood.

Thanks to my tribe, I was able to talk out my feelings and cry as much as I needed to. But eventually I could not avoid their original question: What about getting those new clothes?

There were two issues, really. One was that I just didn't feel valuable enough to give myself something nice like new clothes. The other issue was that I honestly didn't have the money for it. When I was hired as a researcher, I wasn't worried about my wardrobe since I was going to be hiding out in some back office. I thought the salary number Owner-Boss-Lady offered me sounded great. What was that number? $40,000.

I called friends and asked, "Am I under-earning?"

"Possibly," was the answer I frequently heard.

"Is $40,000 a very, very low amount to be earning?"

"Given the cost of living in New York, it probably is."

"Is $40,000 a very, very low amount for a business position where I interview high-powered executives all day?"

"Yup, that sounds pretty low."

"Holy crap, I'm under-earning! I'm an under-earner."

Survival Messages

My story, Danielle's story, and stories like it are so much more common than you think. One of the most important survival priorities for our nervous systems in childhood is to stay safe and nourished with our caretakers.

In ancient times, this meant making sure we were wanted and accepted by the tribe. If we took too much, we feared that the tribe would see us as a burden and eventually throw us out. And for ancient people living in tribal bands, being expelled from the tribe meant dying in the wilderness.

I've heard many people say that there's a stark divide between the messages that men and women hear throughout their lives about this issue. I've read many studies that say that men have an easier time asking for what they want than women do. If I imagine what life was like for our ancestors, I can see how a man hunting meat for the whole tribe would have an easier time asking for what he wants than the woman who prepares it to be eaten. For women in ancient times, the key to survival may well have been to ask for as little as possible in order to ensure the maximum amount available for the hunter man and the children.

Even in more recent times, when husbands brought home the money and wives took care of the home, I can see how the divide continued. But in terms of how it relates to you, right here, right now in the twenty-first century, I've got news for you.

I've known and coached plenty of men who felt anxious about speaking up for themselves, asking for money, asking for what they wanted, dealing with their bosses, you name it. And I've known and coached plenty of women with the same issues. Are the messages different for men and women? Sometimes, very much so. But I'm not asking you to compare yourself to either men or women. I'm asking you to look inside yourself and connect with the value that you bring. Then I'm asking you to connect the fact that you are valuable with the fact that, as an adult human being, you have the right to ask for what you want.

In other words, if you make sure you're bringing good meat and lots of it to the tribe, then it's much easier to see asking for what you want as a win-win situation.

The Win-Win Key to Success

I've heard my support group buddies talk about "under-earning" a lot.

And I've heard many different definitions for the term.

I've heard the very simple version: earning less than you need to take care of yourself.

I've heard the more complex version: patterns of low self-esteem and poor self-care that lead to sabotage at work, sabotage of financial health, and sabotage of career dreams.

And of course, I love the Nora-science (neuroscience) version: A series of fear and self-protection responses that get programmed into our nervous systems to teach us that success and money are dangerous. And because they're dangerous, we need to protect ourselves from them.

Sometimes these patterns come directly from traumatic events that make us feel vulnerable in childhood. Sometimes they come from absorbing our parents' anxiety about their own money and work issues. Often it's a combination of the two. But almost always they teach us that **we can't ask for what we want**.

Not just with money, with almost anything.

So what's the alternative?

I believe healthy abundant earning is based on:

Delivering meaningful, tangible value with service, integrity and honor towards ourselves and others.

When you are delivering meaningful, tangible value with service, integrity and honor, then you are actually **dishonoring yourself and others** if you aren't being paid appropriately for it.

I believe that every human being is capable of delivering unique, tangible value based on a huge batch of gifts that only they can offer the world.

If you're not delivering value, then you're withholding your gifts from the world and you're under-earning.

If you're offering your gifts, but you're not being paid appropriately for them, then you are denigrating your gifts. If you are denigrating your gifts, then you're withholding them from the world (a.k.a. under-earning).

Abundant earning means value, service, integrity and honor on all sides.

It's always a win-win.

It means healthy boundaries on all sides.

It means that all sides get to be human, messy, imperfect, learning and growing.

But here's the kicker. You have zero control over the other side. If you feel like you are in a win-lose situation, then I promise that the biggest opportunity for your growth is to seek out where your nervous system is choosing to "lose." Most of the time, we choose to "lose" because we unknowingly associate winning with danger.

That's the miracle of discovering you're under-earning. It may not feel like it right now, but as you learn more about the tools to come, you will realize just how many choices you have.

Lionel and Martha: Who's Worse?

Lionel was the owner of a taxi and limousine company in a mid-size northeastern city. Lionel was always looking for ways to be more efficient, get his drivers out on more calls, and be a better business owner. He hired me to identify gaps and weaknesses in the business process, structure and company culture so that he could increase revenue and profit.

When I first interviewed Martha, his head of dispatch, she told me some very nasty things about Lionel's behavior. I approached Lionel about this and he fessed up immediately. He knew that he had some issues as a leader, and he was hoping my work could help him grow personally in addition to the business. I've often worked with folks struggling with all manner of difficult behaviors—those who are able to admit to their behaviors and ask for help are far more likely to grow and change than those who blame it all on others. So, yay Lionel!

But here's what Lionel and I were both surprised to find: When I interviewed the individual drivers in the company, they all agreed that Lionel had some unpleasant behaviors that made them uncomfortable. But all of them were much more concerned about Martha. Apparently, every time Lionel mistreated her, she took it out on the drivers. She cursed them out over the two-way radio. And she intentionally sent them to incorrect addresses if they happened to incur her wrath.

If they got lost and she was in a bad mood, not only would she refuse to help them figure out where they were going, she would punish any other driver who tried to help out the lost driver. The lady was out for blood. None of the drivers had been willing to tell Lionel because they knew Martha had far too much power over their livelihood to risk incurring her rage.

When Lionel and I sat down with Martha to discuss her behavior, she was boiling over with blame. First it was all Lionel's fault. Then it was all the fault of her low salary and how it stressed her out. Finally, it was all my fault. It all happened so quickly—Martha was suddenly threatening Lionel, "Your work with Nora is RUINING the company! Either she goes or I go!!"

Lionel looked at me helplessly. He had very little training for this level of blame and rage. Luckily, it was old hat for me. Remember how we don't have to be perfect? Well, here was one of those times I got to practice being OK with my imperfections in front of others.

"Martha," I said, "I know I'm very flawed and I often make mistakes when I'm seeking to guide people and companies to achieve dramatic breakthroughs. But if you tell me, specifically what I can work on, I would love to improve myself and my ability to serve you and the company."

She stared at me for a minute. She didn't have as much fire power if I wasn't willing to defend myself.

Then she figured out her opening. "Well, I want Harold and Skipper in the room because they're the ones who told me the horrible things you've done to me behind my back."

"Oh my God, I would love that! What a great idea!" I replied. "Thank you, Martha for suggesting a strategy that will help us all achieve open, transparent communication much more quickly. I can't wait to hear from Harold and Skipper so that I can apologize to all of you and clean up whatever mess I've made."

Now a strange look of confusion washed over her face. It was as though I had short-circuited her brain. Most people don't expect me to let down my guard when they attack me. How can the fight me to protect themselves if I won't fight back? It was like I was a saber-toothed tiger who had asked her if she wanted a hug.

My behavior seemed so strange to her, it sent her back to blame and suspicion mode. She started screaming at Lionel that I was a lying, cheating, manipulative witch with a capital B. But Lionel could not unsee what he had seen. He fired her on the spot.

Your Turn

What do you think Lionel saw?

I think Lionel saw a very bright lady (Martha) being given the opportunity to deliver her value with service, integrity and honor.

And then he saw her reject that opportunity.

And even though he didn't yet know the ins and outs of Nora-Science, something struck him about me showing up with humility and willingness to grow and Martha refusing to let go of blame.

If you are frustrated and resentful of anyone or anything at your job, I promise you, your resentment is blocking your growth.

Where are you frustrated?

Where are you resentful?

How might your resentment be blocking a win-win situation around integrity, honor and service on all sides?

Not sure yet? Keep reading. I think you'll find more help on this topic.

Self-Care IS Being of Service

Remember how Martha was so eager to place blame? I believe it was because blame is what she did instead of...

- Self-care
- Self-love
- Releasing resentment (because it's not self-loving to stew in misery and resentment)
- Sticking up for her wants and needs with courage and vulnerability

Blame is a defense against the mirage of the saber-toothed tiger we project onto other people.

Self-love, self-care, humility and vulnerability are ways to shatter the mirage of the tiger. They draw us into being of service, regardless of whether or not others are accusing or attacking us.

Think about it. When Martha attacked me, she had no power to hurt me because I asked for her feedback with self-love and honest vulnerability (a.k.a. "Of course I screw up, I'm human! But please help me learn how I can do a little better next time").

Martha didn't want to connect with me. She wanted to stay in rage and blame.

But Lionel told me later that watching me admit my own flaws and ask for more feedback with no shame or fear had given him access to a deeper level of self-acceptance in the moment.

I believe the ability to stand up for ourselves without getting defensive comes from feeling that we are fundamentally worthy and valuable.

When we bring that sense of fundamental self-worth to interactions with others, then we have the opportunity to respond peacefully and positively to any expected or unexpected negative feedback.

Believing in our fundamental self-worth gives us the inner peace to stay calm and embrace feedback which often reveals opportunities for both personal growth and connection with others.

Have you ever had someone take responsibility for something nasty they did without trying to excuse or justify their behavior?

Did you feel closer and more connected to them after they did this?

If so, then you have experienced the miracle of self-love being synonymous with service and human connection. They could not give you that gift of humble ownership of their flaws and flawed actions if they were not also taking very good care of themselves.

Martha needed to disconnect and blame others because her self-worth was so low that blaming others was the only way she could feel safe.

When I offered Martha the gift of mutual honor, I was saying, "I honor your perspective, and I'm honored to have your perspective to help with my growth." Martha's need to blame meant that this offer was too painful for her.

James' Story: Thank You So Much for Telling Me!

James was just starting his career as a real estate agent when we began to work together. His main struggle came from Letitia, the sales manager at his firm. Letitia was extremely high-strung. She was always threatening to fire the agents in the company if they asked for too much of her time, energy or resources. It was strange. You would think she would want to mentor the agents to help them succeed since her salary depended on their success.

Only a few months into his time with the firm, James received a very disturbing email from Letitia. It came after he had asked via email for two different things on the same day—first business cards and then marketing materials for the firm.

James called me when he received Letitia's reply to the second email. It read: "James—your requests have become a terrible drain on my limited time. I'm beginning to think you aren't going to make it here."

Naturally, James was a little flummoxed. He had only interacted with Letitia a few times. It was her job to distribute business cards and marketing materials. Her reply seemed utterly irrational to him. He had already drafted a reply when we talked. It went something like this: "Letitia—I was merely following directions. I am surprised that you would threaten to fire me based on two emails written on the same day. I think it is unreasonable for you to make this sort of threat."

"James," I asked, "do you want to work for this firm?"

"Oh yes, very much!"

"May I ask why?" I was having a hard time seeing him happy in the long-term with a boss like Letitia.

"They have the best listings in SoHo hands down. And SoHo is THE hottest neighborhood right now. If I want to be in the center of things, this firm is where it's at."

"And Letitia? Is she on her way out? She sounds like a handful. Those folks often don't last."

"Oh no, Letitia's high-strung but she's also THE most well-connected listings hunter in the five boroughs. She's got crazy-amazing connections, especially in SoHo. She can get off-market listings that NO ONE ELSE can get. She's a gold mine."

"OK, so if I could give you a way to strengthen your relationship with her, would that be useful to you?"

"You bet!"

"OK, here is the email you write back:

> Dear Letitia,
>
> I am so sorry. Thank you so much for telling me how my requests inconvenienced you. It really helps me to understand how I can respect you and your time better. Please know that you can count on me going forward to be an ally in supporting you any way I can.
>
> Thanks so much for all that you do.

Warmly,

James

"Ooh, I like that," said James. He sent the email, and Letitia's reply came a few hours later: "Thx."

At our next session, I laughed when he brought up her terse reply. "It's a very good sign," I told him.

"Why?"

"Because it shows she feels safe with you. Someone like Letitia will be super charming with clients and super no-nonsense with colleagues. She'll also feel very threatened when she feels like colleagues want to drain the resources she gathers so preciously for her clients.

"She'll be high positive and low negative with clients. And high negative and low positive with colleagues. If she's low positive with you, that means you're beginning to gain access to her inner sanctum."

"Oh, that's good. I want that...how did I do that exactly?"

"You showed up with humility, vulnerability and inner peace when she got freaked out and defensive. By embracing her feedback as an opportunity to deepen your growth without any defensiveness, you created safety and connection for her with you. I think you'll find that she starts to confide in you and trust you in her own way because you just gave her something so precious. You gave her safety in the moment when she expected you to be a saber-toothed tiger."

Tool: Embrace Your Saber-Toothed Tigers

Who are the people in your life who seem to get defensive easily?

Are you one of them?

(I like to keep in mind that, as a human being, I am OFTEN an easily defensive person. That way, I don't get on my self-righteous high horse for too long.)

When others get defensive with you, can you practice saying, "Thank you so much for telling me"?

Or even better, "Oh, I'm so glad you told me that. **Please, tell me more**."

Did you know that saying these sorts of connection-oriented responses is one of the most self-loving, self-caring things you can do?

Even if it feels a little scripted, you will be responding with words that communicate to the deepest threat responses of **your own** nervous system that you are safe.

Would you ever ask a saber-toothed tiger to bite you a second time? No way!

By asking for more negative feedback, you're actually creating new patterns in **your** nervous system that increase your inner sense of peace and safety. If that isn't self-care, I don't know what is!

Can you grab a buddy and practice playing "defensive one" and "safe one"?

Person A can start by hurling a (pretend) insult at Person B. Then Person B can respond with "I'm so glad you told me that. Please tell me more." Then, see where the conversation leads you.

Anything person A says can be met with the "Please tell me more" line and it will only create greater safety for both of you. In fact, you may find yourselves giggling quite a bit. Be sure to switch roles so you can both benefit.

I love this exercise for many reasons, but one of my favorite reasons is this:

Remember how I told you that your nervous system can't tell the difference between your FEAR of a saber-toothed tiger and your FEAR of a Word document?

Your nervous system also can't tell the difference between the SAFETY you create in a practice exercise like this and the SAFETY you create when you use this tool in real life. The more you practice it out loud with other people, the safer you will feel and the easier it will be to diffuse an attack from a person who happens to be triggered into thinking that you are their saber-toothed tiger.

The muscle memory of action and practice is a lot stronger than your thoughts so please, PRACTICE these conversations out loud!

Remember, in order to stop under-earning, we need to: **Deliver meaningful, tangible value with service, integrity and honor towards ourselves and others.**

Do you think that transforming a fear-based defensive situation into a safe, connected situation will deliver meaningful value with service, integrity and honor toward ourselves and others?

Yeah, I think so too.

[For more practice embracing saber-toothed tigers at work, go to www. getaheadandstayahead.com.]

More Nora Story: Learning to Ask for Money

I never thought of myself as an under-earner. I was always terrified around money and had done a bang-up job of having some very low earning years. But to actually call myself an under-earner? This was another matter entirely.

I started calling people every day and saying things like, "I just figured out I'm under-earning. How do I stop under-earning?"

The consensus seemed to be that the fastest way to stop under-earning was to ask for a raise.

Ugh.

Asking the least rational, most explosive person I had ever worked with for a raise was not an adventure I was looking forward to taking. But I had the sense that it would teach me a lot.

I went to the phones and asked maybe a dozen people:

"How do you ask for a raise?"

My favorite answer came from my buddy Bernard. He told me to go to a website where I could look up salary averages (www.payscale.com or www.salary.com are great for this).

135

He instructed me carefully: "Look up the salaries for the titles closest to what you actually do, not what your title happens to be. Find the average in your geographical area and add 10%. And that's the number you ask for."

I did exactly as he suggested. I found the best description of my duties, not my title, and made sure I was limiting my search to New York. The salary number that came up shocked me: $66,000. I was a full $26,000 below average for my area.

However, I was also brand new to the industry, I told myself. But then again, even being new to the industry, I had managed to become my crazy boss's star in three months flat.

I continued following Bernard's advice. Ten percent of $66,000 was $6,600. I purposely rounded down to $6,000 (I was still awfully scared) and added it to $66,000. The number I brought back to Bernard: $72,000. Almost double my salary at that point.

"$72,000? That's great!" said Bernard. It didn't feel great. It felt ridiculous. It felt obnoxious. It felt like Owner-Boss-Lady would fire me just for asking.

"Oh come on, Nora" said Bernard, "what's the worst she can say?" I knew he expected me to say "No," but what I actually felt was much worse.

"Nora, I hate you, you're fired. Oh, and before you leave, I'm going to beat you within an inch of your life."

"Is that something your boss would say or something your mom would say?"

A scene of my mother telling me she didn't want to be my mother anymore popped into my head. It was a scene that had played out many times in my childhood. Good old nervous system. Still protecting me from the saber-toothed tigers of my youth.

"I think this might be harder than I thought."

"Why don't you call people and talk it out until you feel ready?"

Using My Tribe to Build My Sense of Worth

I took Bernard's advice to the letter. I called or chatted in person with dozens of people over several weeks (it took me awhile to feel ready).

And, you know what's funny? About 70% of them actually told me not to ask for the raise.

"I don't know, Nora, you only just started working there a few months ago," said one lady.

("But I've also been promoted to a much more demanding position in those few months," I thought to myself. When I asked this lady how she was doing, apparently she'd been unemployed for several years.)

"Gee, Nora, that sounds scary. Are you sure you should be asking for a raise from a boss like that? It could be painful," said one fellow.

("But pain is the ticket to get on the train," I thought to myself, "If we run from fear and pain, we'll never grow." This was a young man who happened to be in his early 20s with no job, still living in his mom's apartment.)

"Gosh, Nora, I have no ability to encourage you around your career growth. I'm miserable in my own career and probably in a steep decline that ends with getting fired," said one guy.

(The zero-expression tone this guy used as he said this was very creepy. It would be years before I understood that he was probably in a bad clinical depression. At this point, all I thought to myself was: "You're right, I don't want your bad career vibes anyway.")

It was remarkable how, each time I got negative advice, it came from someone who seemed to be struggling with their own money and work situation. Even if that hadn't been the case, just hearing perspectives so contrary to my gut feeling actually strengthened my commitment and resolve to ask for the raise. It was like my Higher Power was using everyone to help me get ready, even the people who thought they were telling me not to do it.

Then there were the positive supportive people. These people fell into two very distinct camps.

The first camp was **The Cheerleaders**. They were all excitement and rah-rah-rah.

"Go Nora! You're such a risk-taker! If anyone can do it, you can!"

"You're scared you're not worth $72,000? Baby, you're worth a million dollars!"

"Oh Nora, I love hearing how brave you are to face this lady. I can't wait to hear how it goes."

About two-thirds of the positive folks were **Cheerleaders**. And, I gotta say, the **Cheerleaders** were very, very nice to have around. It's good to hear pure support and approval. The old wounds heal faster with love like that around.

The second group was **The Warriors**. These were people who told me stories of taking similar risks, feeling similar scary feelings, and discovering amazing results on the other side of the experience.

One man told me a story of how he had told a temp agency that he was looking for temp work that paid at least $30 per hour. They had told him that they never paid more than $18. He had stuck to his guns and a week later they came back to him with an offer of $25 per hour. Eventually he got up even higher. Today, that gentleman has long since left temping behind and has achieved remarkable success, God bless him!

Another woman told me a story of being terribly scared of asking for a raise at the job where she had worked for five years. She was always hearing that they had "no budget." And it had deterred her for a long time. Finally she gathered her courage and presented a point-by-point case as to why she deserved to be compensated for the enormous value she was delivering to the organization. She asked for a 50% raise *and she got it!*

Of the many people I called, only about ten of them fell into the **Warrior** category.

Why were there so few **Warriors**? I don't believe it was because they were smarter or better. They were simply willing to get whatever help they needed to make it to the other side of scary growth. I was trying to be like them.

There were several more stories but the kicker was the last one I needed to hear. It came after six weeks of talking to just over 100 people. And it came from a close friend with whom I checked in on a daily basis.

"Nora, you know what I've been meaning to tell you?" she said one day during our regular morning check-in call. "Years and years ago, I worked for a little property management firm downtown. One day, I realized that I was doing a whole lot more than they hired me to do and I went in and asked them to **double my salary.**

"Really? That's more than I'm asking for."

"I know. And you know what? **They doubled it**."

Out of nowhere, a deep confidence and inner peace clicked into place. It was like someone had re-set my backbone. All my fear and insecurity disappeared. I felt completely at peace with $72,000 as my new base salary. Just like that! A six-week, 100-person, snap of the fingers.

I know you're dying to know what happened for me at work once my confidence snapped into place. And I promise I'll tell you the whole juicy story. But first, I want to help you learn the tools I used to become ready to ask for the raise.

It's important to me to separate the "becoming ready" phase from the "asking" phase because they require two completely different sets of skills.

Most of the people I know who feel disappointed in the results of their "asking" phase are folks who ignored or glossed over the "becoming ready" phase. So, let's make sure you receive the best "becoming ready" tools so that when it's time to ask for what you want (whatever that might be), you've received the support and guidance you truly deserve.

Cherry-Picking

In childhood, we are so wired to seek negative threats that it can takes ten compliments to counteract the effect of one insult. But in adulthood, a mix of positive feedback from people we want to imitate and negative feedback from people we don't want to imitate can help drive us toward healing and learning how to take better care of ourselves.

I talk a lot about the importance of **Building Your Tribe** as you melt internal barriers and heal old wounds. But as you continue on your career growth journey, you may find that people who helped when you were going through a difficult time have a harder time being supportive as you embrace the risks and adventures of bigger and bigger growth.

After all, growth isn't just scary to do, it can also be scary to watch!

When I began reaching out for guidance and support about asking for a raise, it was the first time I encountered a significant portion of my support group tribe who felt threatened, overwhelmed, triggered, or just plain uncomfortable with the fact that I was expressing a hunger for growth.

Up until then, my plight was so desperate that I didn't threaten people very much.

As I continued to grow way past $40,000 per year in income, I found more people who got more uncomfortable with my growth. And these were support groups that were supposed to be all about growth!

Did that mean that all people would get uncomfortable with my growth?

Absolutely not!

It just meant that the next skill I needed to learn was the ability to be selective about which people I talked to and what subjects I brought up with them.

I've heard it said:

"Stick with the winners."

"Surround yourself with people who improve you, not the other way around."

"You are the sum total of the five people you spend the most time with."

I know the intentions of these sayings are to encourage folks to seek out people who challenge them to grow—which is great. However, there's something about these words of conventional wisdom that makes me feel like I'm supposed to be ranking people according to some external chart that makes successful people seem inherently more valuable than less successful people.

Ranking people is a nervous system defense. I'm not into it.

I **am** into using my own internal barometer to check in with myself to see **how I feel** about one person or another. Now *that* feels like self-care.

That internal barometer was especially important when I realized, one day, that I earned more income than the vast majority of people in my support groups.

And I had a decision to make.

Did I only want to talk with people about my problems if they made as much as or more money than I made? That would mean dismissing an awfully large number of smart, kind, supportive, helpful people. And it didn't feel right.

When I first walked into my support groups, almost everyone earned more money than me. It was easy to hear support that felt helpful from almost anyone who'd been around for a while.

Fortunately, as my growth began to turbocharge and my heart told me I didn't want to be a condescending snob, I had to dig deeper for the qualities that made me want to select the people I trusted. I needed people who would embrace my vulnerability, self-discovery and healing because the more my outside life grew, the more my internal need for healing and support deepened.

So, what was it that I was looking for? It wasn't status. Or money. Or fancy titles.

Slowly I began to understand that I was looking for...

- People who have courage
- People who have faced difficult situations and grown from them
- People with curiosity
- People with integrity
- People who are more interested in learning than judging
- People who offer generosity
- People who choose connection instead of criticism
- People who can listen without jumping in with lots of advice right away

- People who like new ideas and new discoveries in both the internal feeling world and the external living world
- People who like to have fun
- People who like to be silly
- People who can laugh

Some people will have many of the qualities above, some just a few. But if they had even one or two, I wanted to welcome that wonderful quality of theirs into my life because I wanted to learn to create and share that quality myself.

As I grew, I found more qualities to look for in myself and others...

- People who seek out inspiration, meaning and impact
- People who are kind
- People who can make me laugh
- People who love business
- People who love growth
- People who are financially savvy
- People who have smart, strategic minds
- People who have great big vision
- People who can get down into the details
- People with patience
- People with a sense of urgency to achieve growth and enjoy goodness in their lives

Obviously, no one has every one of these qualities at all times. But using these qualities as very loose guidelines, I've built a delightful tribe both in my support groups and in the rest of my world. Yes, there are millionaires and billionaires among them. Yes, there are high school drop-outs. And many, many folks in between. But you know what I like best about all of them? I like best how I feel when I talk with them, receive their love and listen to their suggestions.

If you really want people with these qualities around you, seek <u>opportunities to BE a person with these qualities.</u>

Tool: Pick Your Cherries!

Make a list of the qualities of people that you feel good around. Feel free to steal from my list.

Have you noticed some people you used to feel good with who now seem a little threatened as you grow? It's OK, that's normal.

Make a list of actions that you don't like. It might be actions like complaining, criticizing, gossiping, raging, judging, expressing self-loathing thoughts, blaming, avoiding, sabotaging, drinking too much, eating too much, spending too much.

Did you know that you can back away from a person's actions without backing away from the person? Well, you can.

Did you know that you can bring up certain subjects but not others with each person in your life based on how comfortable or uncomfortable you feel around them when that topic comes up?

If It Works with Zeke...

For instance, I'm interested in national and global politics and so is Zeke, a good friend of mine. But even though we agree on many issues, I feel uncomfortable when political discussions come up with Zeke, because I feel like he goes to rage and blame towards the people he disagrees with.

It's actually easier for me to talk with certain people I disagree with who have gentleness and kindness in their style. When I talk politics with them, we have a lot of fun.

But Zeke knows (because I've gently told him) that when we talk, I prefer not to discuss politics with him. Instead, we talk about life, love, art, feelings, friendship, ideas, funny online videos, you name it. But we don't talk about politics, and that's OK with both of us.

[For more cherry-picking tips, visit www.getaheadandstayahead.com.]

More Nora Story: The Ask

Are you ready for the juicy "asking" phase of the story? Well, here it is.

So, there I was, backbone firmly snapped into place, with the newfound certainty that I was 100% worthy of asking for and being paid $72,000 per year for my work.

Then the thought came to me: "OK, great, I feel peaceful about the number but now, how do I actually ask for it?"

I knew if I put a meeting on Owner-Boss-Lady's calendar with the title "Nora Salary Discussion," it would not go over well. She had a tendency toward violent mood swings.

Bringing up money at a scheduled time in the future would make her nuts, I could just feel it.

So, what to do?

Well, you know I'm a spiritual person so I just gave it to my Higher Power. It was pretty simple. I just said out loud (yes, I talk to God out loud sometimes), "OK, God, you gotta show me when to bring this up with Owner-Boss-Lady, because I have no clue."

And I trusted that the moment would be revealed at just the right time.

(If giving something to God feels awkward for you, you can simply choose to relax and trust that your intuition will tell you when the right time has arrived.)

Sure enough, whether you credit God or intuition, the "right time" came in two parts.

The first part happened when Owner-Boss-Lady was in a good mood and paying me a very nice compliment about what a good recruiter I had become. In response, I said, "I'm curious, Owner-Boss-Lady, if a recruiter gets a certain number of placements, is there some sort of reward structure for that?"

She looked me up and down and said, "Honey, you ain't there yet."

And I zipped my lip.

Then, about a week later, a candidate I had found was about to sign on the dotted line for a position that had been a VERY difficult search. It had dragged on for months (which means less profit for the firm).

As Owner-Boss-Lady and I sat in her office working on the last few things that needed to happen for the new candidate to start the job, Owner-Boss-Lady was positively giddy.

"I am soooo happy YOU found Joanne. She is such a great match. She will be soooo happy there. And I am soooo happy to be done with this God-awful search."

Then she looked at me. My face had a neutral expression, mostly because I had learned that expressing feelings around Owner-Boss-Lady could trigger her in the most unpredictable ways.

But at that moment, she decided my neutral expression meant that I was sad.

"Nora, oh my God, you're not happy. You should be happy. Why are you not happy?"

At first, I was going to say something along the lines of, "No, no, I'm happy," and that would have been the end of it.

But in a flash, a little intuitive voice in my head said, *Now! Ask her now!* "All right, God," I thought, "show me what to say."

I started by making a mopey face.

"You're right, Owner-Boss-Lady, I'm not happy."

"I knew it! I read you so well, Nora."

I had to swallow to keep from laughing.

She was oozing care and concern: "What is it, Nora?"

"Well, Owner-Boss-Lady, it's the money..."

Like lightning, she was all business. "We'll talk about it at the end of the day. Not right now. End of the day. End of the day."

"OK." I was calm, sanguine. After all, if God wanted me to wait till 5 p.m., then that's what I would do.

Then her tone changed again—like she couldn't stand waiting ONE. MORE. MINUTE.

"How much do you want?" That was fast, I thought. But I was totally prepared. I had been for a while.

"Seventy-two thousand dollars," I said firmly and clearly.

"Seventy-two thousand???" And she burst out laughing. It was this long, loud, aggressive cackle that shook the walls a bit.

I just sat there calmly. I had no issue with the number or with her reaction to the number because I felt so certain that I was worthy.

Do you know what she did next?

She STOPPED LAUGHING. And then she looked at me looking at her for about a second.

"I can do fifty."

"Deal."

And, just like that, I had gotten my first raise. A 25% raise to be exact. In my fifth month on the job.

The Other Side of the Feeling

It's OK not to get everything you ask for. The growth comes from the actions you take to work on yourself—to learn to believe in your deep value and to speak up for your value honestly and graciously. The results you get just teach you more about the next way you will learn to increase the value you deliver.

If I hadn't done the work to find such a strong sense of peace around that $72,000 number, who knows how I might have reacted when Owner-Boss-Lady cackled in my face?

- I might have run out of the room crying.
- I might have started over-talking and apologizing.
- I might have tried to explain or defend why I deserved more.

There are a million ways I could have sabotaged that conversation.

But what I discovered that I've now taught others countless times, is this. When another person is reacting strongly, staying quiet and present is the most powerful way to get to "The Other Side of the Feeling."

Why do I care so much about the other side of the feeling? Because that's where the magic is. That's where the breakthroughs happen.

Let me put it a different way.

Think of a child throwing a tantrum. Children throwing tantrums don't throw their tantrums because they want to annoy adults.

They throw their tantrums because they are overwhelmed with emotion. Let's be honest, emotions are overwhelming enough for adults. For kids with their tiny little bodies and their wacky nervous systems still in development, emotions are hard.

What kids need most at these moments of emotional overwhelm is an adult who can stay calm, present, loving, and clear on boundaries.

What kids need most to learn from the tantrum experience is that the world outside them can be safe and consistent even when they are feeling difficult feelings.

Most parents don't realize this. Even fewer know how to deliver it.

When Baby Wants Candy...

Let's imagine a scenario that could easily happen in real life. Let's imagine that a child is throwing a tantrum because they are dead set on eating candy for dinner.

Here's a sample list of how most parents respond:

1) You wanna cry? I'll GIVE you something to cry about. You're not getting candy for dinner, you little Brat! (This teaches the kid that having emotions will make the world an unsafe place.)

2) Oh baby, please don't cry, please don't cry. Here, you want candy for dinner? Here have two candy bars. Just stop crying, OK baby? (This teaches the kid that having emotions will make rules crumble and take away consistency and reliability. This condition also makes the world an unsafe place.)

3) Now, little one, be reasonable. Candy isn't good for you. We must do what's right and reasonable. We wouldn't want to give you improper nutrition. (This teaches the kid that feelings are not OK. Only reason and logic are OK. When you feel feelings, stuff it underneath logic.)

I don't believe that any one of these approaches helps children develop the sense of safety, whole-heartedness and respect for boundaries that they all thrive with. I believe the best approach goes like this:

4) Oh, sweetie pie, I hear you that you really, really want candy for dinner. No, you're not having candy for dinner. You're having chicken and broccoli. (Let's say that the kid responds with a pouty face and a refusal to eat the chicken and broccoli. Maybe Mom giggles then gently continues.) Well, unfortunately, if you're not eating chicken and broccoli, then you're not eating dinner. But I tell you what. I'm gonna go set the table now. You let me know if you change your mind, OK?

Simple, loving, present, compassionate, but clear and firm with boundaries, right?

Too few of us actually had parents who knew how to do the #4 response. And I think we're all secretly pining for that experience. It's comforting even as it helps create a sense of safety and reliability that the big rules aren't changing.

If you can deliver the experience of sitting quietly but presently while another person expresses strong emotions, AND if you can be available and ready for open discussion once they've calmed themselves a bit... you will be AMAZED at the power and influence you are able to yield.

Staying calmly, lovingly quiet and present while another person freaks out has helped facilitate an enormous number of breakthroughs in my own life and for my clients.

A few quick examples:

After **Steven** (the CEO of a California venture capital firm) fired his favorite employee for fraud, he was so upset by the situation, that he started screaming about shutting down the whole company, firing me, and calling the police to remove everyone from the premises. I waited patiently till he stopped screaming and said, "You know I think your company has enormous capacity to achieve great things. Would you like me to ask your assistant to start calling recruiters so that we can begin interviewing this guy's replacement? Steven's reply: "Do what the F--- you want." And that was all I needed to help Steven's company begin its next stage of growth.

After **Arthur** (the CEO of a large food company) got a surprise request for a raise that seemed to imply a threat of blackmail from one of his most difficult employees, he told me "Nora you have single-handedly ruined the dynamic of our company." I sat quietly and then asked gently if I could ask a few questions. His reply: "Don't pull any of your mind games on me!" I had to suppress a giggle. "No mind games, I promise," I said. Then I asked him a series of simple questions that helped us develop a game plan for how to respond. We eventually ended up solving the problem.

After **Marjorie** (the CEO of a retail clothing chain) got word that a former employee was suing her company, she called me to say she was leaving the company and shutting it down. I listened for a long while and then asked her if she wanted to keep venting or hear feedback. With Marjorie, the answer was often vent first, then feedback. When her venting was done, we were able to address the issue at hand.

Tool: Be the Safe Parent to Upset People

Let's look at the sample parent responses to the child insisting on candy for dinner again:

1) You wanna cry? I'll GIVE you something to cry about. You're not getting candy for dinner, you little Brat! (This teaches the kid that having emotions will make the world an unsafe place.)

2) Oh baby, please don't cry, please don't cry. Here, you want candy for dinner? Here have two candy bars. Just stop crying, OK baby? (This teaches the kid that having emotions will make rules crumble and take away consistency and reliability. This condition also makes the world an unsafe place.)

3) Now, little one, be reasonable. Candy isn't good for you. We must do what's right and reasonable. We wouldn't want to give you improper nutrition. (This teaches the kid that feelings are not OK. Only reason and logic are OK. When you feel feelings, stuff it underneath logic.)

4) Oh, sweetie pie, I hear you that you really, really want candy for dinner. No, you're not having candy for dinner. You're having chicken and broccoli. (Let's say that the kid responds with a pouty face and a refusal to eat the chicken and broccoli. Maybe Mom giggles then gently continues.) Well, unfortunately, if you're not eating chicken and broccoli, then you're not eating dinner. But I tell you what. I'm gonna go set the table now. You let me know if you change your mind, OK?

Where in your life can you find people to give **you** the loving, present, firm gentleness we all crave in the #4 response?

Did you have that #4 experience growing up at all? Did you have #1, 2 or 3?

Can you start practicing giving the #4 experience to people you encounter who are upset?

Can you start practicing giving the #4 experience to your boss, your clients, and your colleagues? Believe me, it works.

Can you practice with a buddy to make sure you're getting good muscle memory into place?

I want you to practice a scenario with a friend where they pretend to be a difficult person yelling at you. Your job is to simply breathe and pretend they are a child throwing a tantrum who needs someone to keep them company through their tantrum.

Can you and your friend practice switching roles to discover how you each feel as you learn to offer the gentle kindness of listening without escalating while the other person is pretending to get upset?

Then, be on the look-out for a real opportunity to do this with someone freaking out. While you're listening, no matter what they say, do not for one moment take it personally! It's about **their** fear. Don't let **your** fear escalate things. Just keep bringing quiet love to them, as though you were a gentle parent listening to a terrified child.

No matter how it turns out, please talk about it with a friend afterwards. Don't be alone with the experience. Even though I'm giving you a new way to think about it, your nervous system still needs to process the experience with your tribe so that you don't turn your new experience into a saber-toothed tiger.

[For more on bringing the safe parent tool into insane situations or using it to prevent team flare-ups, go to www.getaheadandstayahead.com.]

When the Wheels Come Off the Wagon

Working for Owner-Boss-Lady was teaching me a lot about human beings. But even as I proudly began earning my increased salary, I could see that the wheels were coming off the wagon FAST.

Owner-Boss-Lady had always saved her charm for the clients and her insanity for the rest of us. But now, she was becoming belligerent with clients. One by one, over a matter of months, she lost them. Some she cursed out over the phone. Others simply stopped being willing to talk with her at all.

In all difficult boss cases, I recommend embracing the situation as an opportunity to work on our own behaviors, discover our nervous system triggers, heal old wounds and grow into new capacities. But occasionally, even with all the growth we take on personally, some bosses still have a strong need to sabotage and hurt their businesses and their companies.

I felt that I had achieved enormous personal growth and inner peace with Owner-Boss-Lady. As I watched her hurt herself and the company with her behavior, I realized that I had begun to trust my perceptions and people skills enough to find a healthier work environment.

In the same month that I got the raise, I began to quietly reach out to my network about other opportunities.

As a former recruiter, please allow me to share a few fun facts:

- 75% of all jobs are filled via relationships and networking.

- 13% of jobs are filled thanks to online job postings.
- 12% of jobs are filled through recruiters. Remember, recruiters work for the companies, not the job hunters.

Knowing these statistics, I talked and connected with a wide variety of people—researching what was out there, working with a few recruiters, etc. I interviewed for a number of different jobs but none of them panned out. Thank goodness I had a steady income to give me time to do things differently from the way I had done them when I first accepted the job from Owner-Boss-Lady.

This time, I was committed to getting to know the firm slowly, over time because that's how insanity (or sanity) reveals itself, slowly and over time.

When Others Sabotage

Owner-Boss-Lady was looking for a respite from her pain outside herself in the behavior of others. She didn't understand that her pain came from only one place: her own body.

When you've got a boss in such a self-destructive state that they're cursing out clients, it is perfectly OK to begin quietly taking actions to find a new position.

My advice would be:

- Keep seeking to be of service to your crazy boss;
- Untangle your parent-seeking from them;
- When they attack, practice staying calm and asking for more feedback;
- Stay present as you help them get to other side of the feeling;
- AND do whatever you have to do to TAKE CARE OF YOURSELF.

Remember abundant earning is: ***Delivering meaningful, tangible value with service, integrity and honor towards ourselves and others.***

If someone is sabotaging themselves, you, the business, the clients, then we are not honoring ourselves or their best selves by being party to such negative behavior any longer than we have to.

I encourage you to keep practicing the other work relationship tools in this high-intensity environment. They will create incredible value for you and your growth even while you're looking for another job. You'll be amazed.

Your Turn

Are there places in your life where you think you're observing others sabotage?

What can you do to practice focusing on growth and gentleness when others behave in ways that trigger you?

What can you do to set healthy limits around your time near this person?

What can you do to take action for your own self-care in both the short- and long-term?

The Path Emerges

I spoke to a number of recruiters and applied for a number of jobs as I began to contemplate leaving the job with Owner-Boss-Lady. In fact, I got to the interview phase several times over several months. Eventually, the path to a new job came from my friendship with a wonderful woman I met a few months before.

This woman was a successful recruiter herself in a different area of the industry. And I mean SUPER successful. Let's call her Super-Lady. We initially started spending time together because we both had an interest in writing children's books. But over time, I confided in her about Owner-Boss-Lady.

As Owner-Boss-Lady descended into progressively erratic, unhealthy behavior, Super-Lady helped keep me grounded in the knowledge that Owner-Boss-Lady's behavior was not normal or appropriate.

After months of seeing Owner-Boss-Lady treat clients well even as she terrorized her poor staff, I watched as Owner-Boss-Lady cursed out (and lost) one of her oldest clients. Thanks to the months of building my friendship with Super-Lady, I felt moved to call her for guidance right away.

"I think my boss is starting to take her insane behavior too far," I told her. "I don't know how much longer this company can survive."

By some miracle, after all these months of getting to know each other, this was the moment when Super-Lady said, "I actually have someone I want to introduce to you." It was remarkable timing.

It started with a phone call to a woman who worked for a firm I'd never heard of. Let's call her Lovely-Lady. We had a great talk for over an hour. Was I nervous before the phone call? Of course. Did I check in with friends to get grounded and peaceful? You bet.

Then Lovely-Lady suggested that I meet in person with her partner (let's call him Kindly-Mentor).

Before the interview, I got my calls and prayers in, asking simply for the best outcome for all involved.

When I walked into the meeting, Kindly-Mentor and I had an immediate rapport. I enjoyed getting to know him so much! It turned out he knew Owner-Boss-Lady and her shenanigans quite well so he understood why I was looking to leave. In the interview, I remember that I was careful not to "fake it" or tell him what I thought he wanted to hear.

What did Kindly-Mentor see in me that day? He saw the **meaningful, tangible value** I was committed to delivering **with service, integrity and honor towards myself and others.**

He heard me tell stories of candidates I had found, call numbers I had hit, and searches I had filled. There was no faking necessary. I had done the work to show that I had tangible value to deliver.

A few days later, Kindly-Mentor called and asked if I would like to meet another senior executive in their firm. Let's call him Silly-Fellow. Silly-Fellow had terrific business development skills. He had just brought an enormous batch of searches to the firm, and I would be working with him to help fill those searches.

I had a positive meeting with Silly-Fellow. Again I did all my calls and prayers. During the meeting, I didn't have the same connection with him as I did with Kindly-Mentor, but I think he and I both acknowledged that we would be able to work very efficiently together. Sometimes being on the same page with someone in friendliness but not closeness can be just as productive as feeling close to a colleague.

After my meeting with Silly-Fellow, I realized that it was very likely that I was going to be offered this job. Suddenly money was on the table. Hello FEAR again! (Though maybe not quite as scary as last time.)

Learning to Negotiate an Offer

As I reached out for help on how to be a smart job-offer negotiator, a very savvy friend gave me a set of instructions.

First, he wanted me to decide on the number I was going to ask for. I eventually settled on $75,000. It was an ambitious number to ask for coming from $50,000.

I had told Kindly-Mentor my current salary number even though people are often advised to withhold that information. As recruiters, he and I both had to know every candidate's compensation numbers. To withhold my salary numbers from him would have been strange, to say the least. So, in this situation, I couldn't rely on subterfuge or implication to negotiate for the number I wanted. It would have to be pure honesty and self-worth. Probably for the best anyway—honesty was good for my growth, dagnabbit.

Next, my friend gave me a suggestion I found utterly horrifying. Stomach-turning, Fear-inducing, Horrifying!

Count to Sixty

What was that suggestion? Let's call it "Count to Sixty."

First, according to my friend, when it was time to talk salary, no matter what my future boss might say, I needed to have him say his number first.

(Some companies will ask you for the number you want first. It's been strongly recommended to me numerous times that you want to let the company give their number first.)

Even if he asked me for a number, my job was to refrain from saying mine and simply wait for his.

Now here was the horrifying part.

After he said the number, my job was to count to sixty before I said any words at all. Sixty! Sixty!!! What if he gave me the offer over the phone? Would he think I had hung up?

Sixty—as in 60 seconds. Even in person, what would he think? What if I ruined the relationship right there?

Then my friend talked me through a script of what to say after those 60 seconds had passed. (You'll see it played out in a moment.)

I knew I needed to call people and talk it out a few times just to settle into the fact that I was about to do this very big, scary thing. Yikes! So, that's exactly what I did.

A few days after that, Kindly-Mentor called me and told me they wanted to make me an offer. I was over the moon.

Now there was this little matter of salary. "Let's not talk about money over the phone, Nora," he said, bringing me a huge amount of relief. "Money should always be discussed in person."

We met over breakfast a few mornings later. Here's how it went down...

Kindly-Mentor (KM): Nora, we all really like you and we think we're going to do great work together. We'd like to make you an offer of $55,000 as a starting salary.

And the count begins!

1, 2, 3...

I look out the window. I breathe slowly.

11, 12, 13...

I realize I can make it look like I'm really thinking even though all I'm doing is counting.

20, 21, 22...

I practice looking at Kindly-Mentor like I want to say something but then smile ruefully and keep looking as though I am thinking...I may have been enjoying the drama of the moment just a little more than I expected.

*At about **28 or 29,** Kindly-Mentor speaks!*

KM: You don't have to measure your words with ME, Nora!

I smile at him.

37, 38, 39...

*Finally, **60 arrives**. Making it to the end of those 60 seconds feels so rewarding that I even take a few extra relaxing breaths before I speak.*

Me: Kindly-Mentor, I really want to work with you and your company. But that was not the number I had in mind.

KM: Well, what number did you have in mind!?!?!? (He is practically falling out of his chair with anxiety at this point.)

Me (The soul of calm): $75,000 dollars.

KM: $75,000 dollars?? That's 50% more than you're making now!

Me: That's correct. (I was so calm and present when I said this, it was as if I were saying, "You can do math!" I was amazed at how peaceful I felt.)

KM: Well, I'm going to have to talk my partners about this!

Me: Please do! (Again, this peaceful, connected enthusiasm. It was as if I were saying, "Take your time!!")

A week later, Kindly-Mentor called me and told me that the company's chairman of the board wanted to meet with me. Let's call him Wise-Old-Sweetie-Pie.

(Please understand that I had called multiple buddies every day of that week, not sure if I was ever going to hear from Kindly-Mentor again. This was such a scary process for me!)

My meeting with Wise-Old-Sweetie-Pie was actually really easy and fun. He had a joy about him and a delight in human connection that I found lovely. He didn't have hard-driving questions for me. He asked me where I was from. We talked about New Orleans. I asked him where he was from. He told me about the Lower East Side and the 2ⁿᵈ Avenue Deli.

Our friendly, laughter-filled conversation had gone on for about 15 minutes when he cut me off in mid-sentence.

"Nora, I'm gonna stop you. I asked to meet you today because I wanted to get a feel for you, to see what you were about. And I gotta tell you. I **like** you. You have a pleasant, easy manner and I think you'll be very successful here.

"Well, thank you very much, Wise-Old-Sweetie-Pie. I like you too." He laughed.

"I've been in this business a long time. I started my first recruiting firm back in the sixties. And I've made **a lot of money**. I've had bigger firms, I've had smaller firms. I own three now. It's a good place to be. I know what it takes to make it in this industry, and you've got it, kiddo."

Again, I started to thank him but he cut me off.

"Now, this $75,000 dollar number, is it flexible or is it firm?"

And do you know for a split second, *I ALMOST SAID "FLEXIBLE"!?!?*

But then, my brain shouted "Support groups, support groups!!!" as if to remind me that they were all rooting for me to rock my new salary.

Very matter-of-factly I said, "It's firm."

"All right, then, Nora, it's been a pleasure. Kindly-Mentor will be getting in touch with you."

Again, the waiting! Again, calling my friends for support, staying positive. I prayed for the well-being of all involved constantly. I tried to focus on being of service to Owner-Boss-Lady even as she was losing clients left and right.

I must have written over a thousand times:

Thank you God for my healthy, sane, fascinating, high-paying, abundant job and high salary you send me with grace and ease.

Finally, Kindly-Mentor called. We agreed to meet for brunch on a Sunday morning.

Again, I was a bundle of nerves. My gut told me that counting to 60 was a trick that wouldn't work this time around. I called people to share my fear all week, the night before and the morning of. I was practically in tears on the last phone call I made sitting on a bar stool in the brunch restaurant.

Then I saw Kindly-Mentor walk in and something wonderful happened. My excitement at seeing this person I respected and liked so much became bigger and more powerful than my fear. I hung up the phone and walked enthusiastically over to greet this very special person.

We found a table and the conversation was all pleasantries, weather, weekend plans, you name it. I found myself really surprised and delighted by the fact that I could relax in the present moment and just feel good with this human being. I had spent so much time obsessing and worrying and so much energy trying to replace my worry with positive thoughts...it turned out that **the fear of this moment was filled with saber-toothed tigers but the actual moment was quite pleasant**.

At a certain point, Kindly-Mentor shifted the conversation.

"Nora, I think it's time to talk about money."

"Now, I promise I'm not gonna low-ball you, but before I tell you the offer, I want to make sure you're really coming because you want to work with us and not for the money."

Wow, I was really starting to understand how scary this was *for him!*

"I promise you, Kindly-Mentor, I can't wait to come work with you guys."

"Good. Then let's talk money. I'd like to make you an offer for $70,000 a year in salary with a three-month salary review. Assuming you're performing the way we all expect in three months, we'll bump you up to $75,000. Now, BEFORE YOU SAY ANYTHING, we're ALSO gonna make you a Vice President. We're giving you your own office. There's medical and 401K. This is a great deal, Nora, and you should TAKE IT!!"

His enthusiasm tempered with anxiety was truly endearing. I found myself saying really gently, "Hey, Kindly-Mentor? You've got yourself a deal."

"Really?!? Terrific!!!" And he gave me a big bear hug.

Everybody Feels Fear

Did you notice in my story that Kindly-Mentor was afraid to **ask for what he wanted**? Most people are, no matter where they are in the rankings.

If you asked Kindly-Mentor if he was feeling fear, would he have been able to tell you that he was? I don't know. I think most people go straight to their defenses when they feel fear—and I think this makes nerve-racking moments harder, not easier.

The difference for me was that my defenses were so dysfunctional that I was forced to learn how to identify them as the symptoms of fear. And when I was able to connect with my fear, I learned to reach out to my tribe as much as I needed so that my defenses couldn't hurt me or other people.

But remember how I said that self-care IS service? By getting the nurturing and support I deserved to help me through my fear, I was able to bring a high level of peace and gentleness to my interactions with Kindly-Mentor. And I was able to use that gentleness to connect with him in a way that served him and me, even as we were on opposite sides of the negotiating table.

Your nervous system lies to you that you can't ask for what you want. But if you actually reach out for the love, support and validation you deserve, you will see that asking for what you want doesn't have to be scary at all. It can just be something you do regularly as part of honoring yourself and others.

Does the definition of healthy, abundant earning make a little more sense now? Here it is again:

Delivering meaningful, tangible value with service, integrity and honor towards ourselves and others.

The Physical Symptoms of Nervous System Protection

For the next few years, even though I felt much more confident asking for what I wanted, I still felt intense physical resistance from my nervous system whenever it came time to ask for what I wanted.

For instance, when it was time to ask Kindly-Mentor for my three-month salary-review, I literally had physical sensations of nausea and feeling faint in the days leading up to the meeting.

As always, I reached out to plenty of friends and got plenty of support.

And, to be perfectly honest, I wasn't experiencing a lot of worry or overwhelming obsession. My experience had taught me that there probably wouldn't be any saber-toothed tigers hiding in Kindly-Mentor's office.

But the old nervous system patterns, programmed in through years of my mom's verbal abuse, had left my nervous system totally short-circuited around every piece of money-related growth.

The good news is that short-circuiting doesn't mean dying. It just means being a little uncomfortable—sometimes more than a little. But it's just discomfort. And it passes.

My salary review conversation with Kindly-Mentor was remarkably short. I don't remember the words all that well. I think he told me I was doing a good job and that he was happy to approve my salary increase to $75,000.

What I do remember is the nausea and head rush I felt followed by his question: "Nora, are you feeling all right? You look like you're about to faint."

"Do I?" I said a little too brightly as I tried to pretend I was fine, "That's funny, I feel fine, but I think I'd like to get back to work."

I staggered into my office, closed the door, and breathed slowly till I had gotten my bearings.

I shared my experience that evening with several Support Group Warriors. They all had similar stories.

Pushing Back and Pulling Through

The physical symptom issue didn't come up for a while after that because there wasn't much money to discuss. Then, about nine months into the new job, it was time to split up the job placement bonuses. I had successfully placed just about every candidate in every search we were working on so I had a lot of bonuses coming to me.

However, I felt scared because there was no set formula for how the bonuses would be distributed. Each bonus had to be negotiated by the team that worked on it.

Negotiating with Kindly-Mentor turned out to be peaceful. He and I had a similar concept of fairness. We had an easy time agreeing on numbers that worked for both of us.

Silly-Fellow was a completely different story. He had also brought in about 12 different very high-level searches that year. So if I wanted to take home the big bucks, he was the one I would have to face.

At first, he drew up his preferred splits for each of the 12 searches, brought me into his office and then told me: "This is how much you're getting, please sign here."

Something in me felt funny about it, but he seemed so certain, I wasn't sure how to say no.

When I got home that night, though, I realized that I felt angry with Silly-Fellow and how he had handled the situation. I called a dear friend who told me it sounded more like I was angry with myself.

The solution to my anger wasn't to accuse Silly-Fellow of being a jerk. The solution was to make amends to myself by sticking up for myself.

The next morning, I went to talk to Kindly-Mentor about the situation.

"I felt like he tried to coerce me to agree to numbers that were just way too low for my comfort," I told Kindly-Mentor. Kindly-Mentor said he would look into it.

A few days later, Kindly-Mentor told me that he and Wise-Old-Sweetie-Pie had convinced Silly-Fellow to look at the numbers again with me.

This time, Silly-Fellow had raised each of my splits by about one or two percentage points. It did not feel like much of a difference.

In those intervening days, however, I had had some time to prepare myself. I checked in with my favorite Support Group Warriors and got all kinds of encouragement and advice.

The best advice I heard focused on sitting down with Silly-Fellow, affirming our work together, affirming our relationship and voicing my discomfort with the action, not the person (in this case, the action was making my percentages so low).

I sat in Silly-Fellow's office feeling enormous discomfort and nausea while I practiced breathing and talking very slowly so that my words could be separate from the physical sensations of my feelings.

After Silly-Fellow showed me the revised numbers (which I still found too low), I took a deep breath and said, slowly and deliberately:

"Silly, I love our working relationship. I want to continue working collaboratively with you. I am uncomfortable with the numbers the way they are."

Then he gave me all kinds of reasons why he deserved so much more money than I did. When he was done, I said:

"I hear you. Silly-Fellow, I love working with you. I think we make a great team. I'm the one who found every single one of these candidates. We wouldn't be getting paid if I hadn't found them. I am uncomfortable with these numbers."

Then he gave me more reasons why the number splits he had made were very generous on his part.

Again I affirmed our relationship and voiced my discomfort.

It went back and forth like this for a while. I was keenly aware of the physical sensations of nausea and achiness that I felt around sticking up for myself. But I was also picking up on how uncomfortable Silly-Fellow was. And I was noticing how much his discomfort triggered even MORE discomfort for me.

It was hard enough to go against my deprivation programming and stick up for myself. But then to sit through my uncomfortable response to **another person's discomfort** without trying to take it away from him—that felt like emotional judo.

It was also oddly empowering. The experience of tolerating my discomfort in response to Silly-Fellow's discomfort piqued my curiosity. Silly-Fellow was a person I liked and wanted to keep working with.

How could I learn to stick up for myself without disregarding the relationship?

I discovered that learning to tolerate my already present discomfort AS WELL AS my uncomfortable response to his discomfort was essential to resisting my urge to agree to numbers I felt were unfair.

The Silly-Mentor negotiation was by far the longest and most growth-filled negotiation experience I have ever had.

Altogether, he and I had three meetings over four weeks where I kept affirming him, affirming the relationship and voicing my discomfort with the numbers.

By the third meeting, I felt like an old pro at feeling discomfort without trying to make it go away. In that third meeting, Silly-Mentor finally said to me, "Nora, I just don't think we can resolve this alone. I think we need to get Wise-Old-Sweetie-Pie involved."

"I think that's a really good idea," I said.

I actually had no clue about whether it was a good idea or not. Although it was great to practice tolerating all this discomfort, I had started to feel as if we were stuck. I was grateful for the learning, but I was ready to move on to the next lesson.

Wise-Old-Sweetie-Pie met with both Kindly-Mentor and Silly-Fellow together. Then he met with me.

"Nora," he told me, "I've been pushing Silly-Fellow hard to get him to raise these numbers. He can be pretty stubborn...but then again, SO CAN I! I know that we want to keep you happy because if you're not here, then the work doesn't get done. So I want you to look at these numbers..."

I took a look. They were lower than I wanted but much higher than before.

"Nora, can I be honest?"

"Sure."

"I think you should take this deal. I think you did a great job standing up for yourself, but you're only gonna push him so far, and you do want to keep working with him, right?"

I knew he was right. After all that growth and all those physical discomfort symptoms, the numbers were very much improved. Patience had helped, but now it was time to sign on the dotted line and let go.

Later that day, Silly-Mentor and I shook hands and agreed there was no bad blood between us.

Then he said, "Now, let's get back to work!"

To which I replied, "I couldn't agree more!"

Remember, healthy abundant earning is all about delivering meaningful, tangible value while honoring ourselves and others. It doesn't mean we get everything we want when we want it. I brought honesty and honor to the picture by sticking up for myself instead of stewing in resentment. But now it was time to appreciate what had been accomplished and get back to delivering value to our clients.

Tolerating the Discomfort of People We Like

When you're working with people you like and respect, sometimes it can be harder to stick up for yourself than with people who strike you as crazy.

All those good feelings of collaboration and fun and productivity are really special, right?

So, why would you want to ruin it with some obnoxious hard-driving negotiation?

The answer is that if you DON'T stick up for yourself, over time your resentment will boil over, and YOU will become the difficult one in the relationship.

In order to prevent disintegration, you have to be honest and clear about what you want, **even though you may not always get it.**

It's not about getting what you want, controlling the outcome, or being right. It's about **having the right to be truthful about what you want and how you feel.**

Your nervous system won't let you feel safe in any relationship if you feel like you have to hold yourself in. If you do enough of that holding in, eventually you'll be performing what you think the other person wants and needs. And, your lack of honesty will hurt the relationship.

Even if the other person is being honest about themselves, if honesty is missing on your side, neither one of you will be able to healthfully negotiate solutions because your negotiations won't take into account the full set of issues. The missing issues will be <u>**your thoughts and feelings**</u>.

What ultimately leads to a better resolution is being gentle, honest, open-minded and grounded in the knowledge that no one controls results. Most people are afraid to be honest about their thoughts and feelings because they think honesty is confessing to the thoughts that say, "You need to change for me to be OK."

If you tell someone they need to change, you're attempting to control outcomes and results. And control is a defense mechanism the nervous system creates when you're in fear.

The antidote to fear is not control. The antidote to fear is love and support from people who don't have a personal stake in the situation you find scary.

Once you have the support you deserve from outside work, you can bring courage to speak up for your desires at work with gentleness and without accusing others of any wrongdoing. This is an action with unknown results. You won't know the results of this action until after you've taken the action and the responses to what you've said actually come out of the other person's mouth.

Communicating honestly and gently without knowing HOW the other person will respond can be one of the scariest experiences of human life. And yet, with the right support, it is our BEST bet at healthy relationships in business and in life.

With the right support, the nervous system is happier with honesty than the illusion of control. Honesty is about your feelings, your internal truth. The illusion of control is always a fear-based survival response.

You are allowed to feel relieved to know that none of us is in control, that striving for perfection or control is a fool's errand. When we can be humble about the fact that we're all just stumbling along, seeking progress, we have a much bigger chance of having a great time and achieving some serious success.

All relationships require negotiation. If you practice using these principles with money and work, I promise it will improve the relationships in every area of your life.

Your Turn

Where are you striving for control?

What would happen if you gave yourself permission to offer gentle, honest communication without trying to figure out how the other person will respond?

Where are you not speaking up for yourself?

Could you give yourself permission to practice voicing your desires while reminding yourself that it's OK not to get what you want?

It's our childhood nervous system logic that tells us that if we don't get what we want, we could die. In adulthood, not getting what we want is rarely so serious. Once we know that we'll be OK either way, it's SO MUCH EASIER to ask for what we want.

[For more tips on speaking up for yourself courageously and without the need for control, visit www.getaheadandstayahead.com.]

Lie #8: The Problem Is the Economy

In 2006, when the stock market and the economy were at an all-time high, I managed to get fired from three jobs in six months and earn a total of $11,000.

However, in 2008, as Fortune 500 companies were falling apart at the seams and "the economy" was tanking, I earned over $125,000, more than 10 times what I earned in 2006.

You've just read how I did it. But did you notice that I made no mention of the economy until this page of the book? Does it surprise you to hear that I paid way more attention to my own thoughts, words, actions and relationships than I did to any media coverage of the economy?

Let me assure you, no news story, no media interview, no set of statistics has to take away your success.

Remember, your nervous system wants to find saber-toothed tigers wherever they may hide. Where better than the big monster under the bed called the economy?

Have you ever touched the economy? Have you ever been inside the economy? Does it have legs, wheels, fur, or scales? Does it serve water or wine?

What if the economy is just a big scary idea made up of millions of words, experiences, people, and companies?

And if it's just a big scary idea, then it's perfect for imaginary saber-toothed tigers, right? Because how can you ever know for sure if one isn't about to jump out and eat you?

Lisa's Story: You Don't Understand How Tough Things Are in MY INDUSTRY

"But Nora," said Lisa, "I'm applying for jobs across the country, in one of the most competitive industries in the world. How am I even going to get myself noticed?"

Lisa was about to finish an advanced degree from a very prestigious graduate school when I met her. She was convinced that she would never find a job in her highly competitive, ever-changing industry.

So I gave Lisa the following perspective on economic history:

Industries, markets and demand curves all shift and change over time. In the nineteenth century, blacksmiths were as important to horses for transportation as car mechanics are now. In the 1930s, typewriter companies were at the forefront of business technology.

So, if you're in an industry experiencing a major shift, then, hey, I totally feel your pain. BUT it's no reason that you can't earn great money and love your work.

Why? Because millions of factors cause markets to shift and change all the time.

The notion that there was ever a time when a market, a product, or a set of skills was a sure thing is an illusion. The folks who seek ways to deliver value **as things change** will always have an easier time earning money than those who assume that change is a threat to an established stable reality.

There is no such thing as an established stable reality. Not too long ago, that "sure thing" of yours played the role of upstart, displacing some other "sure thing" earlier in time. You just weren't around to see it.

Some say things would be different if we were living in "the old days" when life was slower and less defined by technology and fast-paced market changes. I disagree. When farmers went to sell their harvest at the trading post, certain crops would be more in demand than others because of unpredictable changes in weather, disease, and all sorts of other factors. Those agricultural markets were always shifting unpredictably.

I once worked for an organization called The Hunger Project that used business training and leadership coaching to help people living on less than a $1 per day in rural Africa, Latin America and South Asia. What did they help them to do? They trained them to become business and community leaders who built simple village-run structures that alleviated hunger and food shortages in their communities within five years. These folks were all subsistence farmers with no electricity just like "the old days" when life was slower in the U.S. and Europe.

As the organization helped these folks achieve self-sufficiency and self-determination, one of the most important principles they taught was creativity and innovation. What does that mean for a village of farmers? It means experimenting with new planting techniques to see what makes for better crop yields in all kinds of conditions. Now, in over 1,000 rural villages across the world, farmers experiment together to find new ideas that will make their farming better.

If you want further proof of the unpredictability of the "olden days," go watch some episodes of *Little House on the Prairie*. There's always some farming emergency where Pa has to come up with a creative way to protect the crops as a bad storm nears. Or some farmhand is coming up with a new way to chop wood that's gonna make a few extra bucks.

The ability to notice things changing and to respond with flexibility, creativity and a commitment to problem-solving is as important for running an old-fashioned farm as it is for having a successful career in the twenty-first century.

Back to Lisa...

"OK," said Lisa, "I think I hear you telling me that it can't be as bad as it seems, but I've sent out over 100 résumés and I haven't heard one peep in response."

"Well, that makes me awfully curious to see your résumé, Lisa."

When she handed me her résumé, I immediately saw the problem.

"Lisa, your résumé lists your duties and responsibilities under each job before grad school. Nobody cares what you were hired to do. They care about what you actually did."

"But this is how university career services told me to write my résumé."

"Mm-hmm. And how many people does your career counselor actually hire per year?"

"Very few?"

"As a recruiter, I built teams at blue-chip companies across the country. I'm telling you, the most compelling résumés list tangible, numbers-based results in bullets focused on achievement, not responsibility."

"But in some of these jobs, I wasn't responsible for any numbers."

"No, that's not possible. Everything we do is quantifiable with numbers. 'Wrote more than seven position papers. Supervised 12 volunteers. Worked on four cross-functional projects covering 18 departments.' Everything you've ever done has numbers baked into it somehow. Your job is to figure out where the numbers are and get them down on paper."

"Why?"

"Because people reading your résumé are busy, overworked and tired. They've got **LAZY EYES**. They're not actually reading your résumé. They're barely skimming. Numbers will jump out at them in a way words won't. Plus, numbers make achievements feel real and verifiable in a way that words simply don't."

"Will rewriting my résumé be enough to get me a job?"

"Probably not. Listen, 75% of jobs come from networking and relationships. Only 12% come from recruiters. And only 13% come from online postings. You need to get yourself into conversations with people who will fall in love with you and want you in their organization."

"How do I do that if where I want to work is 3,000 miles away?"

"You get on the phone, my dear. And then you focus on making people feel listened to, understood, validated and valued. Focus on building relationships from a place of generosity, not desperation. And never let someone's words that they don't have anything for you right now mean anything about the economy or your industry. Just keep networking and creating great experiences for people as they meet you. Believe me, someone will want that fabulous spirit in their company."

When Lisa wasn't freaking out about finding a job, she was incredibly funny, warm, personable and fun. We sat for an hour helping her re-train herself to focus on a few different things from what the career counselors had told her.

Then she was off to the races. It was like she had permission to be her true self and she loved it. Within a short time, she had a job lined up and was moving across the country. No one at her school could believe things had moved so easily for her in such a "difficult industry."

But she knew why. And now you do too.

Rick's Story: Maybe the Economy Just Doesn't Have Jobs for People over 50

When I met Rick, he had been unemployed for 26 months after spending 22 years working his way up to a very high-level job in a large global company.

"Nora," he said, "I just don't think there are jobs out there for people like me anymore."

"People like who?" Rick was a man in his early 50s. I know many men and women his age and older who have great jobs they enjoy.

"People over 50, people not hip to youth culture, people like me. The economy is changing too quickly."

"Rick," I began, "would it be OK with you if we put the economy on the shelf for a minute, and we just focused on your actions and experiences?"

"Maybe if we talk through interviews where you didn't get the job, we can find changes you can make in yourself—rather than obsessing about how 'the economy' is keeping you from success."

As we talked through his interview experiences, it became clear to me that Rick was not particularly friendly in interviews. It wasn't because he was an unfriendly person. It was because he was so focused on making sure the interviewers thought he was smart and accomplished that he forgot to be warm and personable.

Rick had worked 22 years for one company. His nervous system had been trained to feel relaxed and successful in thousands of business meetings over the course of those years. But in those meetings, his top priority had been to find solutions to problems and help his colleagues implement solutions.

When he walked into interviews, he took the same tactic. But he forgot that when someone is interviewing you, they're not just looking to understand how you solve problems, they're looking to know if they'll like being around you—maybe for years to come.

When I asked Rick about his relationships with colleagues, he spoke fondly of the strong bonds he'd built over many years. But even within his organization of 22 years, the most frequent criticism he heard was that people experienced him as brusque in the first few weeks they knew him. Once time had passed, his colleagues grew to see a warm and generous side of him, which they embraced.

As an executive with that fancy company, he had worked on these communication and connection skills for many years. In fact, as we started to talk through these connection skills, he asked me, "What could you possibly teach me that I haven't learned already in the dozens of leadership courses I've already taken?" My answer was, "If you've already learned everything you needed to learn, why are you still in a situation that you don't like?"

None of these courses trained Rick on how to create instant warmth and generosity from the first few moments of an interview with a stranger at a new company. Even though Rick had learned to bring more warmth to his communication as a gainfully employed person, his nervous system reacted differently to the stress of the job hunt and the interview process.

Job hunting is always stressful. It's easy for our nervous system to see saber-toothed tigers everywhere because we see our survival at stake every step of the way. Rick was particularly stressed out. Being unemployed for 26 months had drained his savings and taken a toll on his family life.

"I'm feeling more pressure than ever," he told me. "I need to get a job to support my family. I try to look like I've got it all together, but I actually feel really anxious about how long it's been and how embarrassed I feel to be unemployed this long."

"Rick," I said, "first, I want to congratulate you. By sharing your difficult feelings with me, you're already lowering the defenses your nervous system raises when it feels stress. Those defenses are telling you that your discomfort is coming from out there—from people, situations, **the economy**. As long as you perceive the problem as over there, you won't be able to do much about it. But even though putting the focus on ourselves is the key to growth, it can still be painful to feel the feelings hiding underneath your defenses."

"I want you to know I hear that it's been hard. I've been unemployed and scared too. And it can be **so** stressful. Do you hear that you're not alone? That I'm kneeling beside you?"

Rick nodded. I continued, "And there is hope, I promise."

I began to explain what I thought might be happening in his interviews. "I understand that you love building connectedness with others. But it sounds like it took effort to learn to show your warmth for your colleagues in ways that they could feel. Would you agree?"

"That's a pretty fair way to put it."

"In interviews, most people don't realize that the stress of the job hunt makes us much more likely to revert to old protection behaviors, even when we've spent time learning to behave differently and use new skills. So I think you might not be being as friendly with your interviewers as you would be with your colleagues."

"Of course not! They don't want me to..." and then he trailed off.

"They don't want you to...what, Rick?"

Rick paused and then said, "Fake it, maybe?"

"Do you feel like you'd be faking if you went out of your way to be friendly with interviewers?"

"I guess I do."

"That sounds to me like you see the interviewers almost like they're your enemies. And even though you have to fight them, you're an honest enough fighter that you won't lie to them about how much they make you miserable."

"Is it bad that I do feel that way?"

"Feelings are never bad. It's important that we honor how we feel, even as we're growing past the situation that triggers those feelings. I can see how after 26 months of feeling judged and rejected by interviewers they might feel like your enemies."

"Yeah."

"So, no shame, no blame. BUT we're not just here to talk out your very important feelings, we're also here to get you results! Right?"

"Right! How do I change the way I deal with interviews?"

"Well, first, I want to ask—you hired quite a number of people when you were at your old company, right?"

"Yeah, but that was easy compared to this."

"OK, I hear that your recent stress is giving you a little amnesia about how it felt to interview people. First, interviewers are doing interviews because they need help. Some piece of work is too much for them or their team. They don't take joy in making job candidates miserable—they're trying to fill a very particular gap."

"That's pretty true, actually," said Rick. He had hired a lot of people at his old job so it was fun to watch him realize that he had personal experience to confirm my assessment.

"Next, they need to know that the person who fills that gap is someone they won't hate seeing every day for the next few years. They need to believe they'd be OK sitting next to this person on a plane for business travel or working late into the night on a big presentation. They need to feel like being around you will make them feel better, not worse."

"Oh. Ohhhhh. Ohhhhhhhhhh."

"If you interviewed someone who was very competent but who also seemed like they would make a drama out of anything that went wrong, would you hire them?"

"Absolutely not."

"I picked that one because people who have to work to show feelings usually get uncomfortable with over-showiness of emotion. So that's one that I thought would be an easy one for you"

"Mmm." Rick gave me a sourpuss face.

"But there are also a lot of interviewers who get uncomfortable with people they think are withdrawn or unfriendly."

"So you're saying that I need to go in there acting like they're my old friends even though I barely know them."

"Don't you hope that you will get to know them? That they will become your trusted friends and colleagues?"

"You know what, yes I do!"

"Then you need to show them what it will feel like to have you as their friend."

"Nora, I have an idea. What if every time I go to an interview, I tell myself that the interviewer is my brand new **friend for a day?** I'll treat them with the enthusiasm and warmth that I show my closest friends, and I'll let answering their questions be filled with warmth, not just smarts."

"I like it, Rick. And, please remember, your nervous system may still get stimulated with the anxiety that comes naturally before an interview. This anxiety can affect you physically. So, even as you're guiding your mind to see your interviewer as a friend, remember to slow down, take your time, take deep breaths, and really listen."

"Oh, that's right, I don't just show warmth with my friends. I listen and relax with my friends."

"Exactly. It's not a bad thing to take pauses, listen and consider your words in the interview. In fact, those actions convey a healthy thoughtfulness, especially when your nervous system's anxiety speeds up your speech without you realizing it."

Rick only needed a few more sessions after that. Within a few weeks, his interview style had completely changed to warm, friendly and thoughtful. And within a few months, he had a new job that he loved.

Emily's Story: I Want Big Fish But...

Emily was a successful sales rep for a national payroll company. Her sweet spot was small and medium-size companies. She came to me because she felt stuck at an income level that was good but not great. As I asked her questions about what could be stopping her, it became clear that she was spending the vast majority of her time chasing and serving tiny clients where her commission would be small. She agreed with me that it was time to go after the "big fish" clients where her commission would be larger.

Her biggest fear was that big fish clients would demand that she drop everything to serve them no matter what time they called. And she felt overwhelmed by her obligation to serve them—as though once they wanted something, she was powerless to negotiate on behalf of her own needs or even her own schedule.

"If it's hysterical, it's historical," I told her. This overwhelming fear of being taken hostage by the needs of others sounded like a child in a home with childish parents. Sure enough, Emily had a bruising story of childhood home life—complete with alcoholic parents and constant family drama.

"Emily," I told her, "many people with difficult family histories feel overwhelmingly obligated to help others even if it means they harm themselves."

"Yes!" she exclaimed, "I had to be the caretaker for my parents, even if it meant hurting myself!"

I gave her the "Untangling Parents and Bosses" tool (p. 83) since it also applies to "Untangling Parents and Clients." And I gave her the Comfortable/Uncomfortable Game (p. 91) to help her practice awareness of her needs and feelings.

"Why do I need the Comfortable/Uncomfortable Game, Nora?"

"Because the way we make it OK to harm ourselves by helping others is that we avoid awareness of our feelings wherever we can. In childhood, avoiding feelings is an important survival mechanism so that we don't fight back against our difficult parents and get ourselves thrown out onto the street—who knows if we would survive out there? But in adulthood, the only way to learn how to help others in a healthy way is to learn to know our feelings so that we can honor our own needs as well as the needs of others."

Then I had her practice a version of "Tolerating the Discomfort of People We Like" by pretending to be a "demanding" client and giving her the tools to honor them while still taking care of herself. I like to call this tool:

Setting Boundaries with LOVE

After I'd explained what she could do, here is what our practice round sounded like.

"Emily!" I began, pretending to be a difficult client, "I need you right now, right now, right now!!!"

"Oh client!" she responded warmly, "I'm so glad you called! And I can't wait to help you. I'm in the middle of something right now, can I call you back when I'm done? Does 2 p.m. or 3 p.m. work better for you?"

"How about 5?"

"Actually, 5 works just fine. I'll call you then."

We practiced several versions of this. I had fun being overwhelmingly demanding and over-dramatic. Emily just kept greeting me warmly and calmly and then letting me choose from a few different times when we could talk.

After several rounds, Emily was exhilarated. "That's all it takes? I just embrace them and make them feel really important before I give them choices for when I'm available to help them?"

"Pretty much."

This simple, win-win strategy seemed to open Emily's eyes to the fact that she could pursue and serve bigger, higher-commission clients. We made a plan for her to reach out to 10 Big Fish prospects per weekday until her next session.

After four days of her new commitment, Emily sent me this email:

Hi Nora—

I'm having a hard time reaching the goal of speaking to 10 Big Fish prospects each day. The industry used to be a lot less competitive when I found my bigger clients years ago. Back then, it was really about timing. I don't want to make this into an excuse not to do the work. I'm just wondering if the goal should be to reach out to 10 new prospects each day, regardless of size?

And there it was—the economy, the industry, the pricing—showing up in her brain, giving her reasons to avoid her growth.

Here's what I wrote back:

Hi Emily,

Great job reaching out for help! And congrats on feeling a little stuck! That means you're taking risks and trying new stuff. Whenever we take risks and try new stuff, we encounter all manner of things we don't always know how to handle. The key is to ask for help ASAP rather than letting our stuck-ness stop our progress. I'm really proud of you for reaching out!

First let me say regarding your email: Great questions! Remember that it's normal to get lots of no's when you're reaching out to numerous prospects. The "reasons" these folks are no's are usually what ties sales folks up in knots. I think it's great to listen to the "reasons" in ways that will help you be more strategic. But remember, the reasons people give you for the "no" could change at any moment for any reason.

"The industry is more competitive than it used to be" is a "reason" I hear from salespeople a lot. You NEVER have to buy the "story behind the no." It's just a story. That's all it is. People's brains have a compulsion to make up stories and give reasons. The

truth is that you may not have lower rates than their competitors, but you may have better service, friendlier people, or a more personal touch. People make spending and business choices for a million different reasons that have everything to do with how they experience value. And creating an experience of value takes very different things than what most people (especially salespeople) think.

So, just keep reaching out to those big fish, no matter what story they tell you. You're doing so well!!

Emily's reply came almost immediately.

Hi Nora,

Thanks for your invaluable feedback. Yes, I can definitely see that I'm coming up with a lot of reasons and excuses—I don't want to get stuck in those forever. I will continue to push through and make more contacts.

And just like that, the industry, the economy and all the other big, bad monster reasons Emily's nervous system was using to explain the discomfort of hearing "no" became less powerful as she reached out to new clients and prospects.

How Scarcity Shows Up

Rick's brain, Lisa's brain and Emily's brain told them that some economic condition or a specific industry was a saber-toothed tiger. But for Rick and Emily, their brains also told them that the people who could give them the resources they needed to survive had saber-toothed tiger qualities.

I believe our nervous systems see more saber-toothed tigers around us when we are afraid that there isn't enough to go around.

And it doesn't just affect nervous job candidates or fearful sales people. It affects job interviewers and potential customers. That feeling of desperation, of not enough, creates a sense of pressure and scarcity that ***EVERYONE FEELS***.

Think about it: Don't you feel uncomfortable if a salesperson follows you around a store pushing you to buy things?

I don't think it's because sales or purchasing is inherently stressful—and I used to have panic attacks when I went shopping! I think the moment one person in a conversation about money brings a sense of desperation, pushiness, fear or neediness, then all the people in the conversation get uncomfortable.

That's because our nervous systems are trained to pick up on indications of scarcity. If we start to get the sense that there won't be enough berries or meat for the whole tribe, then we're going to want to guard the berries or meat that we do have.

Our nervous system survival protections don't know the difference between **the feeling of scarcity** from ancient food shortages and **the feeling of scarcity** that occurs when a salesperson gets pushy or a job candidate seems desperate. We just flip right into protection mode around whatever it is the other person seems to want.

In our modern times, when we're in the middle a shopping mall or an office where we're having a client meeting or interviewing for a job, the feelings of scarcity that show up don't make sense the way they did in cave times. Think about it. In ancient times, people might have fought over the last piece of meat in the cave. But, have you ever seen people fighting over pens or staplers during a job interview?

Our nervous systems will tell us that our difficult feelings have to come from some powerful saber-toothed tiger, right? Maybe one that's hiding in the bushes, since everything in this office or this store seems remarkably calm compared to the wilderness.

So where does our scary sense of scarcity go? Oh, it must be that elusive ghost—the economy.

And once we've got the economy in our heads as our big, bad saber-toothed tiger, we can spend days, months, even years obsessing about it.

This obsession blocks our success because thinking about these fears gives people the feeling that they're purposefully and proactively dealing with an important situation. But I don't think finding things to be scared about actually changes much of anything.

How Safety Saves the Day

I've seen many people unknowingly bring a sense of scarcity and desperation to their job hunt or their sales efforts. I've seen these same people alienate their potential employers or potential clients time and time again. But they don't see the problem as the fear that they feel.

They see the problem as "there must not be enough for me" (aka economic scarcity). After all, that's the thought they're having when they're bringing desperation to interactions with potential employers or clients. Isn't it convenient that their behavior actually helps hasten experiences that prove them right? Funny how the nervous system would rather be right than happy, no? But then again, being right about an actual saber-toothed tiger 9,000 years ago was way more important than finding a way to live in harmony with that big old cat. So let's forgive our nervous systems. They're just doing their jobs.

The thing that amazes me time and time again is how these people—who are fighting for their lives in desperation and rejection when I meet them—have the capacity to turn their whole experience around within a day, an hour, sometimes 20 minutes. All it takes is the right guidance and support.

All it takes is to recognize the thoughts and feelings of scarcity and fear governing their consciousness and then start implementing tools that bring safety, generosity and a sense of abundance to their interactions with others.

So, how do you do that?

Tool: Bringing Safety to Scarcity Situations

Every human being has the capacity to bring scarcity and desperation to a situation in a way that can infect almost about every other person in the room.

AND, every human being has the capacity to bring generosity and abundance to a situation that puts others at ease wherever they go.

So whether you're dealing with an interview, a sales meeting, or even a staff meeting, here's how to bring safety no matter what others are up to.

First, there are two things you need to KNOW:

1) All human beings get scared and self-protective in a heartbeat. It's not the economy. It's not you. It's just the old human survival mechanism.

2) Rapid or long-winded talking, quick movements, and self-promotional declarations can all be triggers for other people's survival mechanisms to suspect that something is amiss. Then they get scared and self-protective.

Next, here are five things to DO:

1) Walk into each interaction with a commitment to discover how YOU can serve THEM. There's no way to know this in advance. The only way to find out is to walk in committed to listening.

2) When you interact with others, respond pleasantly and appropriately to their questions but do everything you can to ask questions about them—about how they got to where they are, about what they love, about things that are working for them, about things that aren't working them.

3) Prioritize listening above all else. Remind yourself that listening is the way to get to know them and help them to feel safe, understood, and valued.

4) When you do talk, come from that place of valuing them and connecting with them. It will help you make sure that you're not speeding up in anxiety.

5) When they do ask questions, offer facts but not opinions about yourself. For instance, if they ask for your opinion on your ability to do "X," reply with an impressive numbers-based result you produced that gives them the chance to draw the conclusion for themselves that you must be really good at "X."

[For more job-hunting tips, go to www.getaheadandstayahead.com.]

Lie #9: If I Succeed, Others Will Fail

Rosa's Story: Can I keep my friends?

Rosa had just graduated from a special manager-training program at her company when she and I began working together.

"I spent so many months creating these deep, wonderful friendships with my colleagues in the program," she told me, "but now we're in a position where we're all in competition for scarce resources: promotions, bonuses, even leadership of certain projects.

"Some of my fellow graduates are already getting promotions and raises while others are falling behind. I feel really conflicted because I'm embarrassed to admit that I feel jealous of the successful ones, AND I feel ashamed of doing better than the ones who aren't doing as well as I am.

"All this competition and thinking about the pecking order leaves me feeling distant from my friends AND nervous about my own chances for success. I feel stuck between wanting to get ahead and alienating my friends."

First, I explained to Rosa that it was really common to have these fears. A lot of folks will tell you it's more common for women than for men, but I've known many men and women who had these issues. Then I asked about Rosa's childhood. After all, I needed to know what saber-toothed tigers her nervous system thought it was protecting her from with all her fear and feelings of being stuck.

It turned out that Rosa had been a very good student in a number of competitive schools, but she struggled to navigate the social dynamics of both her classmates and her home life. In junior high, she had only one or two friends. By high school, she was a loner who barely spoke except in class.

To make matters worse, her two older brothers were not only popular but a little bit cruel to her about her lack of social skills. When she was about 12, they'd taken to calling her "Geek Girl," which continued until she went to college.

In the years since, she had worked hard to overcome her shyness and build herself a number of strong friendships that included a close bond with her eldest brother. In fact, it was something of a victory for this "Geek Girl" to have forged such high-quality connections with so many other people in her management training program.

"It sounds like one of the survival interpretations your nervous system created in childhood was that if you wanted to be successful in a competitive environment, you couldn't have a lot of love in your life, especially from people you wanted to feel close to, like your brothers," I told her, "Rosa, how does that make you feel?"

Rosa thought for a minute. "It makes me feel really sad, and kinda lonely."

"And how do you feel when you think of leaving your friends behind?"

"Really sad and lonely," she said.

"That makes a lot of sense," I told her. "The first thing to understand is that your nervous system needs to make the sadness and loneliness make sense by assuming the saber-toothed tigers it saw in childhood are here with you in adulthood too."

"So the loneliness I felt in childhood is now something my nervous system associates with success?"

"It's possible," I told her. "And it's possible that the fear you have of your success bringing about the failure of others—especially your friends—is connected to that loneliness you felt when you were younger."

"But that still doesn't solve my problem," she said. "If I succeed, others fail. And that makes me feel crummy."

"Understanding how your nervous system created these ideas is half the battle. Replacing the story you heard about success, competition and loneliness is the key to creating your new reality. What if we gave

NORA SIMPSON

that new reality a name? I like to call it: ***My Success Helps Others Succeed!"***

My Success Helps Others Succeed!

If you get healthier, will other people suddenly be sick?

If people notice that you're looking fit and trim, they'll often ask you what you're doing so that they can try it.

Success is like that too. If you excel with integrity, honor and fun for yourself and others, many, many people will be inspired to take a page or two from your playbook. They won't always do exactly what you do, but they may start doing a few things or even one thing that they see you do. And even just that one thing can make an incredible difference in their growth and success.

Janis: You Had Such an Impact on Me

Janis was a buddy in one of my support groups who came in around the same time I did. As she watched my income increase rapidly over time, she began to call me to ask my advice on her own life.

I told her about the way that I called lots of people, did lots of soul-searching writing, went to lots of meetings, cleaned up emotional and financial messes I'd made, and just threw myself into using as many tools as I could to get the support I so badly needed.

I think it scared her a little bit.

She seemed to get pretty triggered in our conversations and before I knew it, I wasn't hearing from her anymore. I assumed I had driven her away. All in all, we only spoke a few times. I'm sure I could have been a better communicator back then.

I've learned a lot more now, though I still make plenty of mistakes. And, no matter what I do, I've come to accept that, sometimes, people just don't like my style or what I have to say.

I've learned that I'm not the right cherry for everyone to pick just the way that only some people are the right cherries for me.

186

Years later, Janis reached out to me. "Nora," she said, "I just wanted you to know how much I value your contribution to my personal growth." I was a little shocked. We hadn't had more than three conversations in the previous five years.

"Back when I first met you and you were doing all those things to turn your life around, you really inspired me. It took me a little while to find the strategies that worked for me, but when I did, I thought of you a lot. Even now, I so often think of you because you were the first person to suggest so many of the things I do now."

"Wow, Janis," I said, "thank you so much for telling me that. That's amazing to hear."

But What about the Triggers?

My experience with Janis is a great reminder that one person's success can be both inspiring and triggering for people. Taking action for your success will scare or trigger reactions in other people in all sorts of ways. Some of them will tell you to hold back. (Remember, dozens of people told me NOT to ask for the raise from Owner-Boss-Lady.) Some of them will tell you that your success or your style is obnoxious, selfish, pushy—you name it. That's their stuff. It's not you. You've got flaws, no question. But you get to own those flaws with love and gentleness—bringing acceptance to the whole shebang.

Not Everybody's Gonna Like You...and That's OK

The converse is true for the trigger-y people. When they bring anger and judgment to you, what they're really telling you is how angry they are with themselves. You don't have to go to your anger and judgment for them. You can love and accept yourself and send good vibes their way. Keep in mind you can do this even though you do not ever have to talk with them if they trigger discomfort for you.

The other day, a friend in one of my support groups called me in tears. I've been mentoring her for a while now, and she had also been getting guidance from a fellow I was close to years ago. Let's call him Buddy. I haven't spoken to Buddy in years but I long ago let go of any resentment I had towards him over the reasons we grew apart.

Apparently, Buddy told my friend that he didn't want to help her anymore if she was getting support from me. This came as a complete shock to me. For many years, I've felt a lot of fondness and gratitude for all the gifts I received from being close to Buddy years ago. I knew he wasn't interested in communicating with me now. (I've reached out a few times.) But he still holds a special place in my heart as someone who helped and guided me in amazing ways. (In fact, he shows up under a different name earlier in this book.)

I told my friend that she had my permission to use my name and let Buddy know that I supported his feedback for her regardless of whatever else he thought of me.

"Not everybody's gonna like you," a wise mentor of mine used to say. That doesn't mean that you've hurt them by being you. It just means that people's nervous systems will see you as their saber-toothed tiger as often as they need to.

Eddie: Sharing Our Victories

Yet another friend of mine, Eddie, used to tell me that whenever he heard me talk about my success, he felt inferior—like a failure. One day, I told him that I understood that he was having difficult feelings. However, when he connected the difficult feelings to me and my success, it made me feel sad and lonely.

Slowly but surely, Eddie began to notice when those comments would come out of his mouth. Eventually he stopped, and it made me feel closer to him. Then one day, he came up to me and said, "Nora, I've been so inspired by your success, and, guess what! I just achieved a whole new level of success for myself this month!"

"Eddie, that's great! I'm so happy for you!"

"I mean it's not at your level but—wait, no, I'm not going there. It's not a competition!"

"Oh, Eddie, it makes me feel so close to you to hear you say that. Can we please take a moment to appreciate your wonderful growth and success together?"

"You bet, Nora!" And then we gave each other great big hugs.

And do you know he never compared himself to me again? We only share joy in each other's victories now. And Eddie and I both continue to grow in our success.

The more successful and visible you become, the more people's nervous systems have the chance to make up that you are one of their saber-toothed tigers. That's OK. The triggered folks have just as much opportunity to learn from their saber-toothed tiger triggers as you do.

So go be your Superstar self! And trust that people are learning and growing in all manner of ways, thanks to you and your success all the time.

Back to Rosa...

"So, my opportunity," said Rosa, "isn't necessarily to change the actions I take for success, but to change my attitude as I take them?"

"Rosa, do you feel guilty about succeeding?"

"Yeah, I think I do."

"And do you feel guilty about taking actions that will lead to your success?"

"If I see a friend struggling to take the same action, yeah, I do."

"OK, so here's what I want you to do. I've got these "6 Steps for Spreading Success" I use to remind myself that my success serves the success of others. Will you listen to them and then consider adopting them as a guide for your own actions?"

"Bring it on!"

The 6 Steps for Spreading Success

Step #1: Accept that I don't know what's best for another person. No matter what my brain tells me, I have no idea if it's better for someone to achieve the goal I'm going for or a different goal. None of us can tell what's best for any of us before it happens.

Step #2: Release control. Trust that my willingness to learn and grow into success will lead to growth and learning for others in ways I cannot predict and cannot control. Remind myself constantly that my success helps others succeed in ways I cannot control or even, at times, understand.

Step #3: Listen to my heart. Focus on taking honest, consistent, high-integrity action to achieve the goals I'm drawn to. Remember that every time I take action toward my success, I improve my ability to serve others' success in ways I cannot control or predict.

Step #4: Get whatever love, support and guidance I need. Love and support should feel easy on both sides. Remember that resisting success-oriented actions means I need more love, support, and guidance, not that I'm doing something wrong.

Step #5: Trust that I'll be guided to the right success for me. Success may not always look the way I imagined it. But I'll know it when I feel it. Open my heart by constantly affirming that I am available for the "better version" my tiny brain cannot imagine.

Step #6: Share the success of my heart and my hands. When people inquire about my success, share my open heart and mind, my commitment to consistent action and growth, and my gratitude and awe at the unpredictable twists and turns of the journey. Most people will be delighted. A few will be jealous. Stay close to the delighted ones.

"So basically, you're saying that if I just keep taking good care of my own actions and attitude, everything else will fall into place?"

"Pretty much."

Sure enough, Rosa began to "go for it" at work. She applied for several different higher-level positions in the company and was offered two different ones that she was able to combine into one higher-paying job.

Then, she was also asked to consult on a number of cross-functional projects initiated by several of her friends in different departments. She also helped implement several new strategies for new business development at the company. Some of these strategies grew her division's profits by quite a bit—which made her look pretty good to her bosses. But several of her ideas actually helped other divisions grow in new ways, which strengthened her relationships with friends and colleagues across the organization.

Tool: Applying the 6 Steps for Spreading Success

I've re-stated the 6 steps below with a few thought-provoking questions to help you apply them in your own life.

Step #1: Accept that I don't know what's best for another person. No matter what my brain tells me, I have no idea if it's better for someone to achieve the goal I'm going for or a different goal. None of us can tell what's best for any of us before it happens.

- Are you feeling guilty about having or achieving something someone else doesn't have?

- Are you sure what you have is what someone else needs? Is it possible they need something else you can't imagine?

- Do you find yourself thinking that you know what another person needs? Can you accept that there's no way you actually know what anyone needs?

Step #2: Release control. Trust that my willingness to learn and grow into success will lead to growth and learning for others in ways I cannot predict and cannot control. Remind myself constantly that my success helps others succeed in ways I cannot control or even, at times, understand.

- Do you spend a lot of time thinking about the right thing to say or do? Do you become anxious or obsessed over these things?

- Do you fear hurting others with your success? Can you allow the fact that you don't know what's best for them to relieve you of that fear?

- Do you find that fear and the desire for control keep you from taking consistent action?

Step #3: Listen to my heart. Focus on taking honest, consistent, high-integrity action to achieve the goals I'm drawn to. Remember that every time I take action toward my success, I improve my ability to serve others' success in ways I cannot control or predict.

- Can you give yourself permission to be honest about your deepest desires?

- Can you have faith that if you feel a strong desire to achieve a goal, then the journey of growth you take to achieve it will be meaningful, no matter what the outcome?

- Can you gently focus on taking tiny actions consistent with achieving your desires?

Step #4: Get whatever love, support and guidance I need. Love and support should feel easy on both sides. Remember that resisting success actions means I need more love, support, and guidance, not that I'm doing something wrong.

- Are you drawn to people who are mean to you? Can you give yourself permission to back away from those people?

- Can you give yourself permission to reach out to the ones you think are super-cool but a little intimidating?

- Can you give yourself permission to reach out to many cool people in order to get the help you need from the few that will turn out to be just the right helpers for you?

Step #5: Trust that I'll be guided to the right success for me. Success may not always look the way I imagined it. But I'll know it when I feel it. Open my heart by constantly affirming that I am available for the "better version" my tiny brain cannot imagine.

- Are you open to the joys and discoveries of the unexpected?

- Can you accept different results from what you expected but still keep taking consistent actions?

- Can you keep asking questions so that you're always learning from your experiences?

Step #6: Share the success of my heart and my hands. When people inquire about my success, share my open heart and mind, my commitment to consistent action and growth, and my gratitude and awe at the unpredictable twists and turns of the journey. Most people will be delighted. A few will be jealous. Stay close to the delighted ones.

- When you talk to others, can you share the open-hearted attitudes that worked for you?

- When you talk to others, can you share the tiny, consistent actions that led to results?

- Can you listen to how you feel as you share with them? Can you take very good care of yourself by sharing more with people you feel good with and less with people you feel crummy with?

Not Enough to Go Around

Even with all these tools for spreading success, plenty of folks still hear their nervous systems saying that there just aren't enough resources, jobs or successes to go around.

It is true that if you get a promotion, someone else may not. Or if it's between you and five other candidates for the job, and you get the job, the five other folks won't.

But does that mean that those people will have failed?

Are the people who don't get what you get, earn what you earn, achieve what you achieve, learn what you learn—are those people failures?

No, they're not.

They're just different from you. Every person has their own path to take. And every person has choices to make.

Did I choose to grow up in a home where I felt scared and worthless? No. Could I have chosen differently? Probably not.

Did I choose to make something of myself anyway? Well, I tried BUT I FAILED!

I failed until I was willing to ask for lots and lots and lots of help, love, support and guidance.

I failed until I was willing to learn to work in a way I'd never learned to work before.

Failure, and the pain that came with it, was actually THE MOST IMPORTANT influence on my journey to find the resources and guidance that helped me turn my life around.

At an individual level, if you try to save another person from the **dignity** of their pain, then you may be taking away an experience that will guide them to far better places than you could dream of for them.

And if you sabotage your own success in the process, then you'll have sabotaged two people's growth journeys, not one.

(Please don't misunderstand me. At the national level, policies that help people lead healthy, productive, safe lives are incredibly important for a successful economy. But I'm not talking about you as a voter or a lawmaker. I'm talking about you as an earner.)

If you're concerned that others are struggling, encourage them to go looking for the love, support, guidance and learning they deserve to make their growth process feel less overwhelming.

You can recommend this book. And, at the end of this book, I've put a list of all kinds of marvelous personal and professional growth resources that you can offer others and take advantage of for yourself.

[For more on the 6 Steps for Spreading Success, go to www. getaheadandstayahead.com.]

More Nora Story: Joy and Grief

Success brings a mixture of feelings whenever it happens. By the end of December 2008, my income for the year was over $125,000. I was 28 years old and I had earned six figures for the first time in my life.

I called Victor, one of my support group friends, to share the news.

"That's fantastic, Nora!!! I'm so happy for you!"

"Thanks, Victor! I'm over the moon!"

We chatted for a few minutes and then we both went back to work.

(What? A personal phone call during work hours? Don't worry, I left the office during my lunch break and called on my way to run an errand.)

But after work that night, I called Victor back. "Victor, can I tell you something? I was feeling good when I called you and I was feeling good during the brief few minutes of our conversation. But as soon as I hung up the phone, I suddenly felt this huge wave of grief. Am I crazy?"

"No, Nora, you're not crazy. I totally identify with what you're saying. I feel joy at my successes and my six-figure income, but it does come with a lot of grief for me as well."

"How so?"

"Well, it reminds me of being told by my family that I was worthless when I was a little boy..."

"Oh sure, I got those messages too," I said.

"And it can make me feel separated from friends who aren't doing as well as me—like I don't belong anymore."

"That is one of my biggest fears around all this," I said. "What if people start hating me because I'm successful?"

"Some of them will," said Victor, "but that's their nervous system programming, it has nothing to do with you."

"Yeah," I said, "and **my** nervous system programming is that whenever I achieved something as a kid, my mom delighted in all the attention she got for it in public. But as soon as we got home, she would yell at me for all the ways my achievement made her and my sister feel inferior. And then she would hang out with my sister and ignore me."

"It sounds like success brought a lot of pain into your life when you were young," said Victor.

"Yup," I said, "and loneliness. It was very lonely in my house for me. I wasn't allowed to be part of the fun that my mom and sister had together.

My sister was just a kid; she didn't know any better. But my mom created an alliance with my sister in this way that led me to believe that if I was going to be successful, then I wasn't allowed to be loved."

"That does sound lonely," said Victor.

"So even when all my dreams come true, I still have to feel pain?"

Victor laughed.

"Pain is part of life, Nora. It will be with us even when we're having our most wonderful times. But I think it's wonderful that you can give yourself the room to feel all your feelings—to really let yourself be a whole person."

"You know, Victor," I said, "I like that. I like that I get to be a whole person."

Saber-Toothed Tigers that Mock Success

It's hard to accept, but the truth is that almost all children get punished for success in some way or another. If you're the smart kid in class, the other kids get jealous and pick on you. If you're the talented one on the sports team, the opposing team will make sure to target you to prevent scoring by your team.

If you've got musical or performance talent, a sibling, a parent, or certain kids at school might denigrate you for it. If you're good-looking, you'll feel the jealousy of others, or unwanted attention from people you don't like.

Many of these experiences might not seem like brutal traumas, but for the children who experience them, they can feel just as scary as a saber-toothed tiger. Why? Because in childhood, your nervous system is looking for saber-toothed tigers so that it can protect you from them.

If athletes on the opposing team, kids at school, parents or siblings seem to punish us for achieving something meaningful, it can give us the expectation that we'll be punished somehow for being successful.

Tool: Grieving the Punishment

It's normal to feel a little scared, sad, lonely, even weepy, when you achieve a meaningful goal. Some of it is the release of the energy and emotion it took to get there. But much of it also relates to those little moments of punishment and mockery when you did something worthy of praise and applause in childhood.

I encourage you to open your heart to those feelings and reach out to your tribe for support as you feel them and release them.

This is super-important for your continued growth because if those feelings get pushed to the side, they'll create a sense of pressure and defensiveness over time that could lead your nervous system to sabotage you by acting like saber-toothed tigers are growling at you when all you're really feeling are old feelings from childhood experiences.

I don't want your nervous system to sabotage you. I want your nervous system to have all the support it needs to lower your defenses, get vulnerable with safe people and discover the deep peace that comes from wrapping your arms around the child that you once were and reassuring her that she is safe even as you achieve success.

You'll want to practice this skill as much as you can because the more you grow and succeed, the more you're going to need it.

As we grow and expand, our nervous systems do best when we experience more support, not less. After all, we're going into further and further uncharted territory. Now, experiencing support isn't just about people who've guided you. At a certain point, it will begin to include people who love and cheer you on, in part because they love **_your_** guidance.

Your Turn

What experiences from childhood did you have where your talent or your success led to mocking or rejection?

How did it make you feel?

What did you learn to use to defend yourself from those bad feelings? Did you hold back your talents? Did you go for it while feeling judged and lonely?

What would happen if you allowed yourself to achieve that thing just out of reach here in the present?

Do you have any fears of losing love or respect if you did achieve that thing?

Do you have any fears of appearing threatening to colleagues or bosses if you achieve that thing?

Can you give yourself permission to feel the fear?

Can you reach out for support from your tribe?

Do you notice yourself feeling jealousy toward anyone else? Could it be that whatever you envy about them is something you haven't given yourself permission to do?

What would happen if you tried doing the thing that makes you jealous of that other person or other people?

What does the fear around the jealousy remind you of from childhood?

Do you see how noticing your jealousy of other people's success gives you a path to self-discovery and growth for yourself?

Can you allow that your success can offer others similar paths even if you have no idea what their childhood stuff is and how they'll heal it?

Nora's Lifetime...

These dynamics are still completely present in my own life. Not long ago, the reliably successful monthly income of my business tripled from one month to the next. I jokingly called it "the 10-year, one month success."

I found myself incredibly excited throughout the month as the money came in, but as I got closer and closer to the triple number, I found myself getting more and more scared. I was getting one-on-one support from close friends, but I still felt a strong sense of fear and grief as this goal became more and more real.

One night, I went to a support group meeting where I felt very safe and shared the actual numbers. There were people I'd helped there and people who had helped me. Most of them were a little of both. When I was called on to share, I couldn't look anyone in the eye. My heart was pounding in my chest. I stared at the floor, said the numbers out loud and then said, "I'm so afraid you're all going to be jealous of me or hate me or something."

Then I looked up. Everyone was smiling and looking at me with love in their eyes.

After the meeting, a bunch of folks came up to me. "You're so brave and vulnerable, Nora," one friend said. "I can't wait to hug you and celebrate with you," said another friend. That night, I received hugs from eight different people. The next day I got a celebratory voicemail from a friend about how happy she was for me and how inspired she felt. I saved it and I still have it on my phone.

It wasn't just me who needed those hugs. It was young child Nora and teenage Nora who felt rejected when she was successful in school or student council or drama club.

I'll probably need those hugs and support for the rest of my life. And I sure am glad that I will. With all the success I've had, it can be easy to forget that I still need nurturing and tribal support. But pain and grief are my best reminders that tribal support is missing. And, somehow they always seem to drive me toward support at exactly the right time. As humans, we do best when we're firmly planted in the middle of a loving tribe—even as we grow and grow and grow to levels we never could have imagined.

Tool: Lightening Up, Letting Go

There comes a certain point in success where all the self-awareness, all the grief, all the tribal support, all the growth has gotten you far enough that you start to see a few things:

1) You'll always be human. As much as you grow, you'll never have this life thing so figured out that you won't make mistakes.

2) Other people will always be human. You can't control their mistakes, their flaws, their jealousies, or even their love and delight.

3) Since you really have no control over the future, the past, other people, and a bunch of your own behaviors, you might as well have some fun along this growth path you've chosen.

Make sure you find people in your tribe you can laugh with. Because laughter and silliness can make even the weirdest feelings and tasks bearable.

When I started this journey back in 2006, I almost never laughed. I was scared of everything. Things in my life felt intense. Gradually, as I began to relax into my new skills (skills like earning money, staying calm around crazy bosses, reaching out for help and finding it available), I began to feel safe having fun again.

For me, that looked like going to comedy shows, watching funny online videos, singing silly songs with friends, learning to crack jokes with friends and with clients.

What could it look like for you? Could you take a comedy improvisation class? Could you watch a funny movie? Could you invite a friend to do something silly and fun with you like laser tag or apple picking or water-skiing?

Life is not a dress rehearsal. We do all this growth and it's fantastic. But we also need to decompress, chill out, and just take time to enjoy. You deserve it. And so do all the people who will learn from your incredible example over the next 2, 10, 20, 50 years. Don't those people deserve to have fun too? It will be easier for them to lighten up if they see you lightening up. And you may not even have met them yet!!

So, go have fun being the Superstar you were born to be!

I can't wait to celebrate all your success!

[And for even more success tools, come join me at www.getaheadandstayahead.com.]

Appendix: Free Personal and Professional Growth Groups

Money and Business Support:

SCORE (Free business advice and mentorship) (www.score.org)

Savvy Ladies (Free financial guidance for women) (http://www.savvyladies.org/)

Dress For Success (Free career mentorship for women) (http://www.dressforsuccess.org/)

Debtors Anonymous (www.debtorsanonymous.org)

Business Debtors Anonymous http://www.debtorsanonymous.org/BusinessDA.htm

The Tools of Business Debtors Anonymous http://www.ncdaweb.org/BDATools.html

Underearners Anonymous (www.underearnersanonymous.org)

New York Debtors Anonymous (www.danyc.info)

Healthy Relationship Support:

Alanon (www.alanon.org)

Free Alanon Phone Meetings (phonemeetings.org)

Adult Children of Alcoholics (ACOA) (www.adultchildren.org)

The "Laundry List" of ACOA (http://www.adultchildren.org/lit/Laundry_List.php)

Survivors of Incest Anonymous (http://www.siawso.org/)

Co-Dependents Anonymous (http://coda.org/)

Sex and Love Addicts Anonymous (SLAA) (http://www.slaafws.org/)

New York SLAA (www.slaany.org)

Yes, there are a lot of 12-step and anonymous groups on this list. If you've never been to a large number of 12-step meetings, done the work to build friendships slowly over time, and **worked the steps with a sponsor**, then it's easy to have a lot of misconceptions about these groups.

The 12-step culture of anonymity is designed to avoid promotion, marketing and fancy names that will hit the right "target market." These totally free groups are filled with well-intentioned, imperfect people who are working hard on their growth. If you're skeptical or turned off by the names of the groups, that's OK. I was too. But I'll tell you—the ones I hated the most (at first) turned out to be the ones that benefitted me the most over time.

If you're interested, great. If not, no worries. There are wonderful people to connect with all around you. Now, go build your tribe!

TRUE DIRECTIONS

An affiliate of Tarcher Books

OUR MISSION

Tarcher's mission has always been to publish books
that contain great ideas. Why? Because:

GREAT LIVES BEGIN WITH GREAT IDEAS

At Tarcher, we recognize that many talented authors, speakers,
educators, and thought-leaders share this mission and deserve to be
published – many more than Tarcher can reasonably publish ourselves.
True Directions is ideal for authors and books that increase awareness,
raise consciousness, and inspire others to live their ideals and passions.

Like Tarcher, True Directions books are designed to do three things:
inspire, inform, and motivate.

Thus, True Directions is an ideal way for these important voices to
bring their messages of hope, healing, and help to the world.

Every book published by True Directions– whether it is non-fiction, memoir,
novel, poetry or children's book – continues Tarcher's mission to publish works
that bring positive change in the world. We invite you to join our mission.

For more information, see the True Directions website:
www.iUniverse.com/TrueDirections/SignUp

Be a part of Tarcher's community to bring positive change in this world!
See exclusive author videos, discover new and exciting books, learn about
upcoming events, connect with author blogs and websites, and more!
www.tarcherbooks.com

TRUE DIRECTIONS
AN AFFILIATE OF TARCHER BOOKS